Technology

Technology

Discoveries • Inventions • New Technology

Contents

FOUNDATIONS OF TECHNOLOGY 6

POWER STATIONS/ENERGY 14

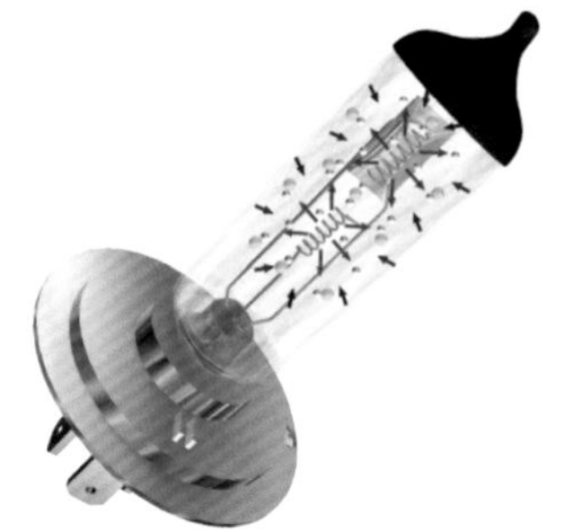

LAND TRANSPORT 26

AIR TRANSPORT 34

CHAPTER 1

Foundations of technology

Today's technological achievements have been made possible thanks to the creativity and thirst for knowledge of many researchers and inventors. The history of technology begins with the history of human beings.

We will never know who it was who first used a wedge, moved a heavy object with the help of a lever, or attached a rope to a bucket to draw water from a well. These devices didn't just simplify and improve the lives of the people who first used them; they became the 'building blocks' that led to other designs and inventions. They are also known as 'simple machines' that transform forces and energy.

Technology took a big leap forward when people began to settle. People had to find ways of managing the newly settled lands to produce enough food from their fields. As people began to keep and breed cattle they invented the plough (approximately around 3000 BC). After settlement in one area for a long time, clay and ore were discovered, and, along with the invention of the wheel, this led to busy trade over long distances. Clay and ore were turned into tools and weapons such as spears, axes, bows and arrows, as well as millstones and earthenware. As trade grew, inventions spread far and wide and were constantly being improved. The foundations or building blocks of technology are the simplest inventions such as the wedge, lever, wheel and also pulley. They are still used today, in a huge variety of combinations, to produce the most complicated vehicles, machines and gadgets.

Wedges

The stone tools made by our ancestors more than two million years ago are among the oldest human inventions. Although there are no drawings or paintings from this time, stone tools found during excavations in the Olduvai Gorge in Tanzania, in East Africa, in 1960 are proof of this. The first axes and scrapers were created a million years later by early hominids. The wedge is the basis of four kinds of tool. Depending on how a wedge is used, it either separates or lifts objects. It is one of the simplest machines there is and is used to transfer force. A wedge has two flat surfaces that form a sharp angle, or, put another way: two inclined planes that are joined at one end. If a wedge is pushed lengthways into something, the use of a relatively small amount of force will have a great effect at a right angle to the planes of the wedge. If an axe is driven into a piece of wood, the wood splits easily depending on the angle of the planes or blades of the wedge. Wedges were also used in advanced civilizations. The largest blocks of stone used to build the Pyramids, temples and other constructions were created using wedges. Wedges were also used early on to mine ores and in shipbuilding, to prop up masts. Before the discovery of screws and threads, individual parts of clocks were held in position with wedges. Today, wedges are used in knives, scissors, axes, saws, files and many machine tools such as moulding machines.

Plough with depth wheel, around 1895

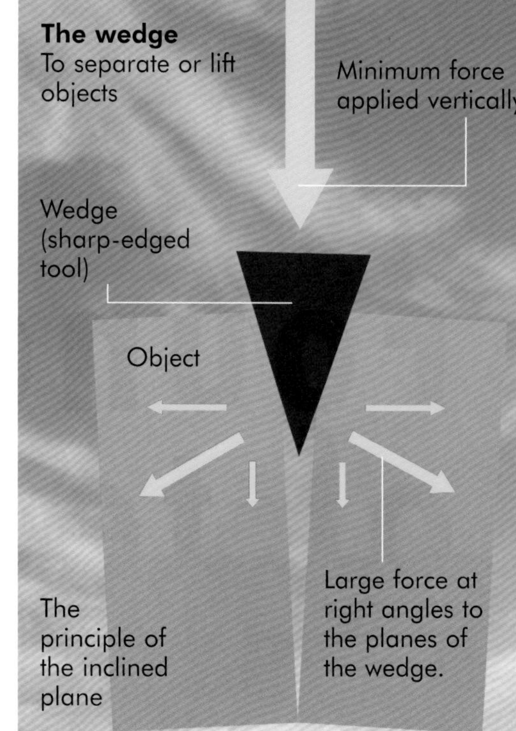

The effect of a wedge. *A small force applied over a long distance (short arrow) results in a large force over a short distance at right angles to the planes of the wedge (long arrow).*

Levers

English wheelbarrow, 1835

The Greek mathematician and physicist Archimedes of Syracuse (approx. 287–212 BC) is credited with explaining the law of the lever. He is supposed to have said: 'Give me a place to stand on and I will move the Earth!' We use levers so often in everyday life that we don't even realise we are using them. When we press down a door handle, use a bottle opener, step on a pedal or push a wheelbarrow, we are always using 'leverage' or the action of a lever.

One of the main building blocks of technology, the lever is a simple machine with which force can be transferred from one point to another. There are two classes of lever. In a Class 1 lever the effort is applied on the same side of the fulcrum as the resisting force. In a Class 2 lever the effort is applied on the other side of the fulcrum from the resisting force. Simple examples can show us how leverage works.

A ***wheelbarrow*** *also works according to the principle of levers. If you apply force to the levers of a wheelbarrow (its handles), the load is in the middle, and the pivot or fulcrum is on the opposite end. This makes it possible to lift the load off the ground and easier to transport.*

In a loaded wheelbarrow, the wheel is the fulcrum or pivot. A force is needed to lift the wheelbarrow (the load) by the handles, its long levers, which are at some distance from the fulcrum. This is how a heavy load can be lifted with relatively little effort. If a large boulder has to be moved, imagine placing a smaller stone somewhere near the boulder. The smaller stone represents the fulcrum. A crowbar can then be placed below the large boulder and above the small stone and force applied at the opposite end of the boulder so that it can be lifted. Here, both forces are at different distances to the fulcrum. The distance between the effort and the fulcrum is called the effort arm and the distance between the load and the fulcrum is called the load arm. According to the law of the lever, the amount of effort required and the load are in inverse ratio to the lever arm. If effort × effort arm = load × load arm, they are balanced.

*A **weighing scale** is a Class 2 lever. The fulcrum is in the middle and the distances between the effort and the fulcrum and the load and the fulcrum are the same. When effort and load are also equal a scale is balanced.*

Pulleys

A pulley is a mechanical device used to raise and lower loads with less effort. A long time ago, people discovered an easier way to lift a load: they attached a rope to the load and pulled the rope over a fixed wheel, a 'pulley'. Using a pulley changes the direction of movement but doesn't reduce the amount of effort you need. So the fixed pulley wheel didn't reduce the effort needed. However, pulley wheels were nonetheless being used over 2,000 years ago. They were used to pull up water from a well with a bucket attached to a rope or to lift heavy building materials. Fixed pulleys are still used today in many areas of technology.

In addition to 'fixed' pulleys there are 'moveable' pulleys, where the wheel is attached to the moveable load. If a load is pulled using a moveable pulley such as a crane, the load hooks can move up and down with the moveable pulley. The effort needed is reduced but the distance the effort has to travel is doubled.

If you use a combination of fixed and moveable pulleys the effort needed is diverted and reduced at the same time. Aristotle (384–322 BC) also made this connection.

If you use a pulley rope with both a fixed and a moveable wheel the force needed is halved but you need to pull twice as much rope towards yourself. The amount of work you need to do is not reduced but the amount of effort needed to pull the load is reduced. If a pulley with two moving wheels is used a quarter of the effort will be needed.

Pulleys used to lift loads

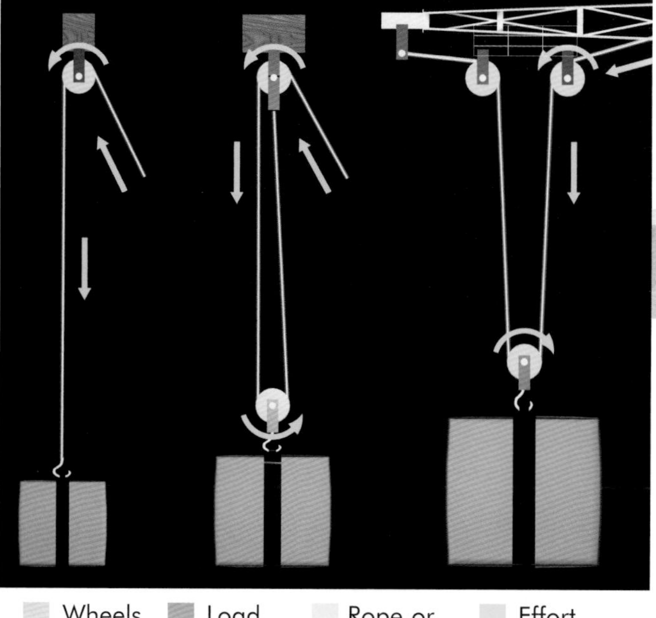

A pulley is a combination of fixed and moveable wheels and is often used to load ships. Most pulleys have two moveable wheels. A fixed wheel is needed to direct the load and effort. Every moveable wheel reduces the load or effort needed by half. So the first wheel reduces the effort needed to move the load by half, but the rope needs to travel twice the distance. Using a second wheel reduces the effort needed by half again. So only a quarter of the effort is needed over four times the distance.

Wheels

Disc wheels were made from the wood of a tree trunk that was rounded by hand. They were not very strong and broke easily. The discovery of fixed axles around which the wheel could rotate was a big step forward. Pegs held the wheel in place on the axle.

Spoked wheels were mainly used for chariots. Their appearance did not change much until the 19th century.

The wheel is one of the greatest human inventions there is because it helps to transfer force efficiently. Many things in industry and technology would just not be possible without the wheel.

No one knows exactly when the wheel was discovered, or who by. We do know that the wheel was used more than 5,000 years ago. In early times, tree trunks were placed under heavy loads to transport them. Later, people began to remove the bark to make the logs smooth to make it easier to roll them. The Egyptians created the first rollers to transport the massive blocks of stone used to build pyramids. In Mesopotamia remains of manmade discs of wood from the year 3200 BC have been found. They were probably modelled on the pottery wheels that had been invented 300 years earlier. The wooden discs were made of several planks joined together make a round object. In later years, two of these round discs were combined with an axle. The Sumerians are said to have used four-wheeled carts as early as 3000 BC. The Egyptians used them much later.

Wheels began to be used in different places at very different times. For example, wheels with spokes were already being used in China in 4000 BC but only became known in Europe in 1500 BC. They were being used in Egypt in 1600 BC. The use of spokes made wheels lighter and faster. Spoked wheels were usually used for two-wheeled chariots.

Spokes were sometimes made of bronze. To make the wheels stronger, a rim was created by wrapping leather bands around the wheel, or by using broad nails, and later iron and bronze rings were used.

Spoked wheels are still used today. In bicycles they are usually made of metal with very thin steel spokes attached to the rim. In heavier vehicles, like vans or buses, the spoked wheels are made of cast steel. The spoked wheels of passenger cars are usually made of sheet steel with gaps to help cool the wheels. Combinations of light metal castings are also used. Wheels are essential for motion in many things and in many aspects of technology, such as wheelbarrows, rolling mills, lathes and gears. Many machines and gadgets would be impossible to make without wheels.

The first tyres

In 1888 Ire Dunlop invented the air-filled tyre. He first developed it for the bicycle because his son used to suffer from backaches from cycling. Tyres helped to reduce his back pain.

Threads and screws

Threads and screws are also simple machines. They are inclined planes with a spiral shape.

A screw is made up of two parts: a shaft and a thread. Screws either have a round, triangular or rectangular cross-section, depending on what the screw is used for. Wood screws have a conical shaft and metal bolts for machines have a cylindrical shaft. The distance between the two threads that lie one above the other is a screw's incline. The Sumerians and Egyptians were using wooden threads as early as 2500 BC, but metal screws were first made 1500 years later. To make a metal screw, a wire was soldered in a spiral onto a metal bolt. Screw threads of different sizes began to be used to fix and join many gadgets and machines from the 15th century onwards. Making a thread in early times was an expensive and time-consuming process, so they were only used sparingly. In the middle ages, metal threads were made with the help of files, and wooden threads were carved. Pliers were used to turn screws since screwdrivers had not yet been invented. Around the 17th century the first cutting tools or 'dies' to cut external screw threads were invented. The dies had to be made very precisely, so that screws and threads could be produced uniformly in large quantities and could be used for different things without each screw needing a specially fitted thread.

An Archimedes screw, invented by Archimedes of Syracuse (287–212 BC), is a special kind of screw used to pump water upwards.

Apart from being used to fix and connect things, 'micrometre screws' can be used to make the finest adjustments with forward and backward movements. Screw threads are also used to make zoom adjustments to a camera lens and to lift car wheels with a car jack.

Metal screw

A **corkscrew** is also an inclined plane with a spiral shape. Some corkscrews are actually two simple machines combined: a spiral (screw) that is twisted into the cork and two levers used to pull out the cork.

The Archimedes screw

An 'endless screw' used to drain and irrigate fields can be turned to pump water upwards without moving forward itself.

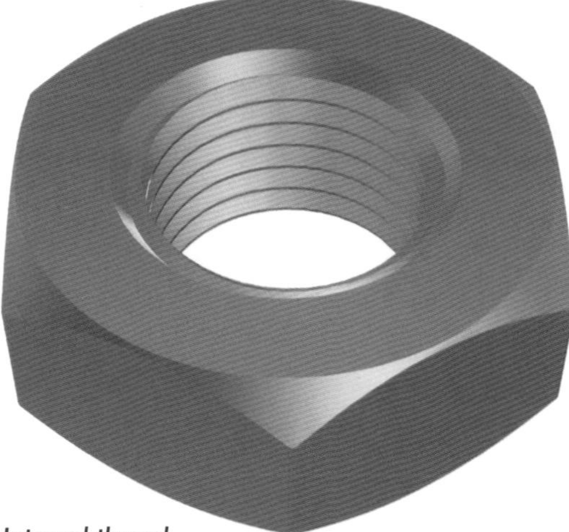

Internal thread

Nuts have an internal thread of groves in the centre to use with fixings, which can be loosened and tightened again. Both right-hand and left-hand threads are used.

External thread

Bolts have an external thread whose grooves have to be precisely enough for it to fit in the inside thread of a nut.

Cogwheels and gears

Gears are used to transfer or multiply a movement or force. A gear consists of at least two cogwheels. A cogwheel is a wheel with several 'teeth' of equal size around its edge. The teeth make it possible to turn and transfer movement from one wheel to another without friction.

*In a **bevel gear** motion is transmitted at a 90° angle and the two wheels turn in opposite directions. Bevel gears are often used in milling machines, printing presses or farm machinery.*

No one knows when the cogwheel was invented; however, objects similar to cogwheels were used in ancient Greece around 250 BC. Around the same time, the ancient Egyptians were using waterwheels with wooden rods placed at particular angles to each other.

Early mathematical calculations for cogwheels date from the 17th century, and cogwheels began to be made in the 18th century. From the mid-19th century machines for the manufacture of cogwheels (moulding machines) were invented.

Force and motion are converted by using gears. Speed and torque (rotational force or moment of force) can be converted by using a combination of friction wheels and cogwheels or drive belts and pulley belts.

If you have two cogwheels, the driving wheel and the wheel being driven move in opposite directions. If both wheels have the same size they will move at the same speed. If the driven wheel is bigger than the driving wheel it will rotate more slowly. If the driven wheel is smaller it will rotate faster. Using cogwheels of different sizes makes it possible to achieve a lower or a higher speed. You can see this at work in bicycle gears. In cars, different gears have to be engaged according to torque and speed. Even though we use the same word to describe this mechanism in a car, car gears

Shaft

Waterwheel

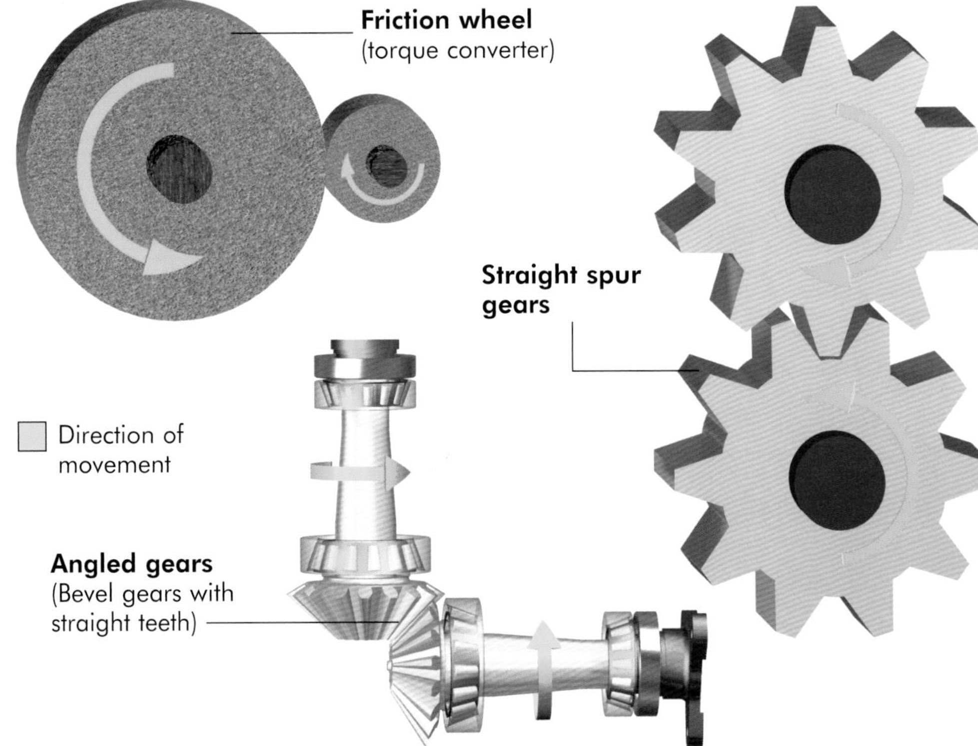

The gears are made up of several interlocking cogwheels of different sizes connected by a gear lever. In more modern mechanisms such as the car, the teeth are helical (cut at an angle) to make gear changing smoother and quieter. Old-fashioned 'crunching gears' have become 'synchronised'. Angled bevel gears and worm gears are almost always use for hand-operated machinery. The steering column of a car is one example. The axle drive of a car is now known as a planetary gear system. The gears are connected via the drive shaft to the gear motor that has been designed as a differential gear. The driving and driven wheels in gears move in opposite directions.

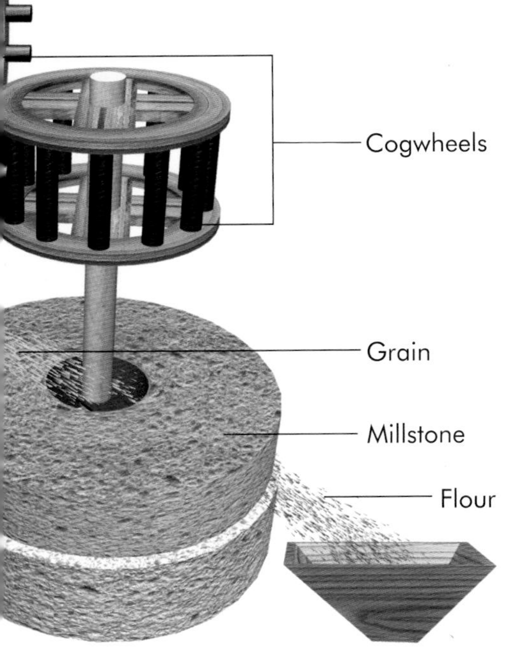

are much more complex.

Cogwheels can be made of all kinds of different material, for example, cast iron, steel, other metals, synthetic materials or wood. There also many different kinds of gears. In spur gears, for example, the teeth can be either straight or slanting and on the inside or the outside of the wheel rim. We also use bevel or worm gears. Whatever the gear, to ensure continual movement, all of them will have at least one pair of interlocking cogwheels.

Even the flour mills used by the Romans consisted of a system of vertically stacked wooden cogwheels that were driven by a waterwheel.

Friction

Friction is the force that has to be overcome when two objects in contact with, or touching, each other begin to move. Wherever solid surfaces slide or roll over each other, friction is acting on them. Friction always results in a loss of energy because it works against movement. It also always generates heat.

Car brakes are a good example: they work by making use of friction. The braking mechanism of disc brakes, shoe brakes or multiple-disc brakes acts against movement by converting the energy of motion into heat or by cancelling it.

Ball bearings placed in vehicle axle bearings are used to reduce friction with the help of lubricants.

Sledges are another useful example in understanding friction. If you want to pull a sledge over a flat surface you need a lot of effort to get it moving. To keep it moving you need to keep using effort, if you let go of the rope the sledge comes to an immediate stop. The moment you pull the sledge rope tight, you can already feel a strong counterforce, known as kinetic friction.

Friction is greatest just before either of two objects begins to move. When a sledge begins to move a counterforce known as kinetic friction acts on it, making it difficult to move it. Kinetic friction is as strong as the pulling force being used to pull a sledge. The kinetic friction has to be constantly balanced with the force being used against it to avoid the sledge coming to a stop. On a flat surface, the static frictional force of an object is always greater than its kinetic frictional force. So, if two surfaces are lying on top of each other, they are more easily separated by the use of either a small lifting force or a kinetic force.

Static friction makes it possible to walk on flat or inclined surfaces and to hold screws and nails in place. Two objects slide directly over each other when friction is dry. When friction is lubricated a lubricating film of liquid separates the surfaces of the two objects from each other. There is no friction within the layer of liquid.

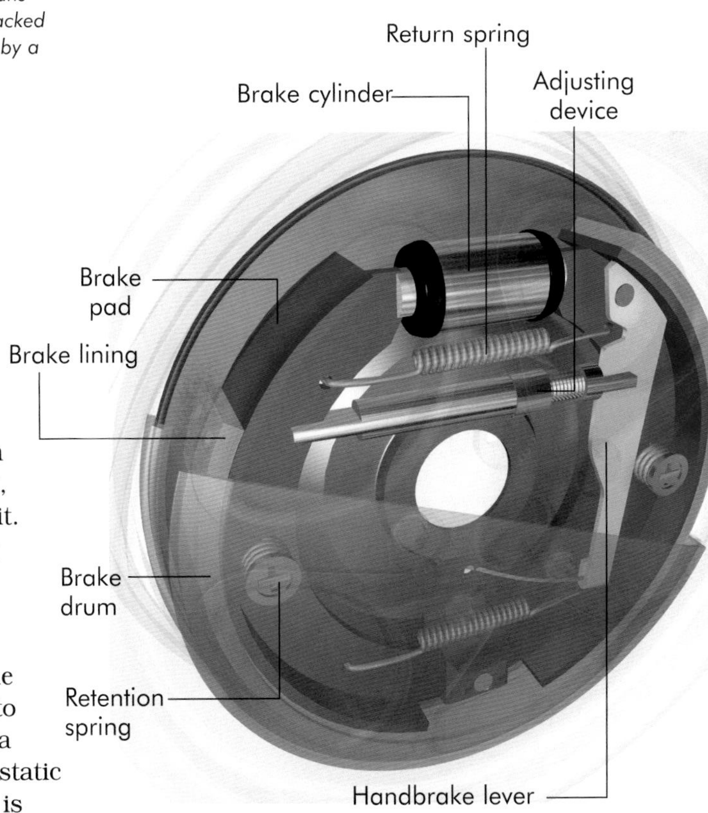

We make use of friction in car brakes. In a drum brake the brake pads are pressed against the brake drum through a wheel brake cylinder the moment a driver presses the brake pedal. The pads and drum slide against each other and the wheel's kinetic energy (energy of movement) is converted to heat.

°C

CHAPTER 2

Power stations/energy

Energy is the capacity to do work. There are many different forms of energy, including thermal and light energy, nuclear energy, kinetic energy, potential energy and chemical and electrical energy.

One of the most important topics of our times is the earth's finite energy reserves. This relates to sources of energy such as natural gas, oil and coal. Until recently they used to be the most widely used sources of energy. Earlier still, the physical power of human beings and animals was used, and, to a lesser extent, energy from wind and water.

These sources of energy were not enough for the rate of industrial development. After numerous experiments, from the mid-18th century onwards, the first steam engines were made for use in flour and textile mills, ships and railways. The most revolutionary ideas came from Great Britain.

Although the first experiments with electricity were conducted as early as the 17th century, the electromagnetic coil was only discovered at the start of the 19th century. Electricity then became a new source of energy. Early steam engines were gradually replaced with electric motors that could generate more power and were also smaller.

The discovery of nuclear fission, along with the realisation that nuclear energy could be used to create electricity, provided us with another form of energy from the early 1950s. However, nuclear power goes hand in hand with the danger of radioactive fallout. For this reason, nuclear power is seen as a controversial source of energy. Alternative and natural sources of energy such as solar, wind and hydro (water) power are being developed.

Batteries

Current flow in a battery

Negative terminal
Anode
Cathode
Battery casing
Lamp
Cathode
Anode
Sulphuric acid (electrolyte)
Sulphuric acid (electrolyte)

Secondary or accumulator batteries use the chemical reaction that occurs between two electrodes immersed in electrolytes to create a current. As soon as the circuit between them is closed, the electrons from the positive electrode (anode) flow to the negative electrode (cathode). An electric current can be maintained as long as this exchange of electrons takes place.

Batteries create electrical currents and produce electrical energy by electrochemical means. Rechargeable, 'accumulator' batteries can be recharged again and again, but non-rechargeable batteries with 'primary cells' are burnt out when empty.

An Italian physicist called Volta was the first to show that an electrical current is created when two different metals (e.g. copper and zinc) are put into certain conductive chemicals (electrolytes). The reactive cell created is also known as a galvanic cell. In 1800, Volta created the forerunner of the electric battery, the 'voltaic pile'. A direct current can be created from the chemical energy in such a cell, and the electromotive force produced is known as 'voltage'. A battery is made up of several cells put together. A car battery is an accumulator or secondary cell, which is continually recharged by a generator when the engine is running. Car batteries usually have six cells, each including plates of lead and lead oxide immersed in diluted sulphuric acid. The lead plates are connected to a negative terminal and the lead oxide plates to a positive terminal. As a battery discharges electrical energy, the lead, lead oxide and sulphuric acid are turned into lead sulphate and water. When the battery is recharged this turns back into sulphuric acid.

The different sized batteries used in torches or watches are usually primary cells. They do not contain a liquid but a dry chemical paste (e.g. ammonium chloride) and are covered in an insulated steel coating to prevent leakage. A carbon fibre rod and zinc housing make up the electrode, and this explains why they are called carbon–zinc batteries. They were invented in 1875 by the French chemist Leclanché.

Batteries with electrodes made of mercury or silver are more powerful, however. Lithium batteries are particularly long-lasting and can be stored undamaged for long periods.

Although batteries are efficient and powerful, many of them have a great disadvantage. The use of chemicals such as mercury, nickel or zinc makes them harmful to the environment and they must be disposed of as hazardous waste.

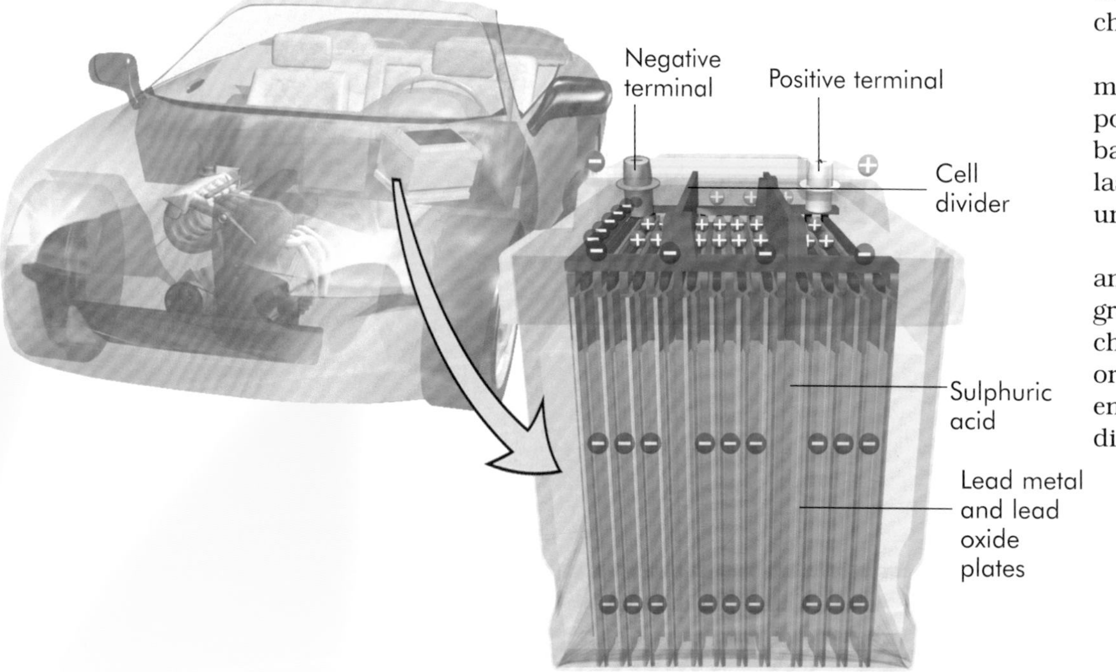

*A conventional 12 V **car battery** has six series-connected 2 V cells. Each cell has electrodes made from negatively charged lead metal plates and positively charged lead oxide plates immersed in diluted sulphuric acid acting as the conductor. When a current is produced, the positive hydrogen ions and negative acid ions migrate to the terminals and complete the electrical circuit.*

Light bulbs

The light bulb continues to be the most common source of electric light. A light bulb works by making use of the heat produced by electric currents. Two hundred years ago, the first step towards the invention of the light bulb was made when electric current was used to heat a length of wire until it glowed white hot. This showed that when something is heated to a very high temperature it can produce light and thermal (heat) energy. The knowledge behind this principle was used to invent the light bulb. In 1854, the German Heinrich Göbel, an American immigrant, invented the first usable light bulb. It consisted of a carbonised bamboo fibre in a vacuum-filled bottle. Over the next few years, J.W. Swan from Great Britain replaced the bamboo fibre with one made of carbonised cotton coated in diluted sulphuric acid. In 1879, after several experiments in the Edison Electric Light Company, Thomas A. Edison began to make light bulbs based on Göbel's invention, and at the same time W. Siemens produced light bulbs based on Swan's idea.

Today, light bulbs are made using material that can withstand high and fluctuating temperatures as the filament heats up and cools. Light bulb filaments are made of tungsten, and are extremely thin, allowing them to get white hot (about 2500 °C). The tungsten filament is wound in a coil to obtain the maximum amount of light in a relatively small glass bulb. The ends of the filament are joined by a wire, which is fed through a glass fuse and connected to electrical contacts in a screw cap. To prevent the filament from burning out at high temperatures, the oxygen in the bulb is replaced with a noble gas – argon gas is usually used. When the current is switched on, migrating, electrically charged particles collide with the tungsten atoms, and the tungsten filament heats up and radiates light. The thermal energy created in this process is much greater than the light energy produced. Approximately 95% of the electrical energy is converted into heat and only 5% of the electrical energy is converted into light.

These kinds of light bulb are now banned in many countries since they are not energy efficient and are therefore harmful to the environment. Energy-saving, compact fluorescent bulbs are used instead. Here, the current flows through a gas in compact fluorescent tubes and produces light without the heat.

Noble gas or vacuum

Tungsten filament wound in a coil

Screw cap fitting

A typical energy-saving light bulb: the compact fluorescent bulb.

Electrical circuit

Source of electric current

Electrical circuit switched on

When an electrical current is switched on the filament begins to glow. However, it cannot ignite because the glass bulb has no air. Bulbs with high wattage have short, thick filaments, while bulbs with lower wattage have long, thin ones. More recently, fluorescent tubes, which use less electricity and are more luminous, are increasingly replacing bulbs. Direct current (DC) light bulbs are more luminous because they operate on a lower voltage at a higher current to obtain the same wattage, since Volt × Amp = Watt.

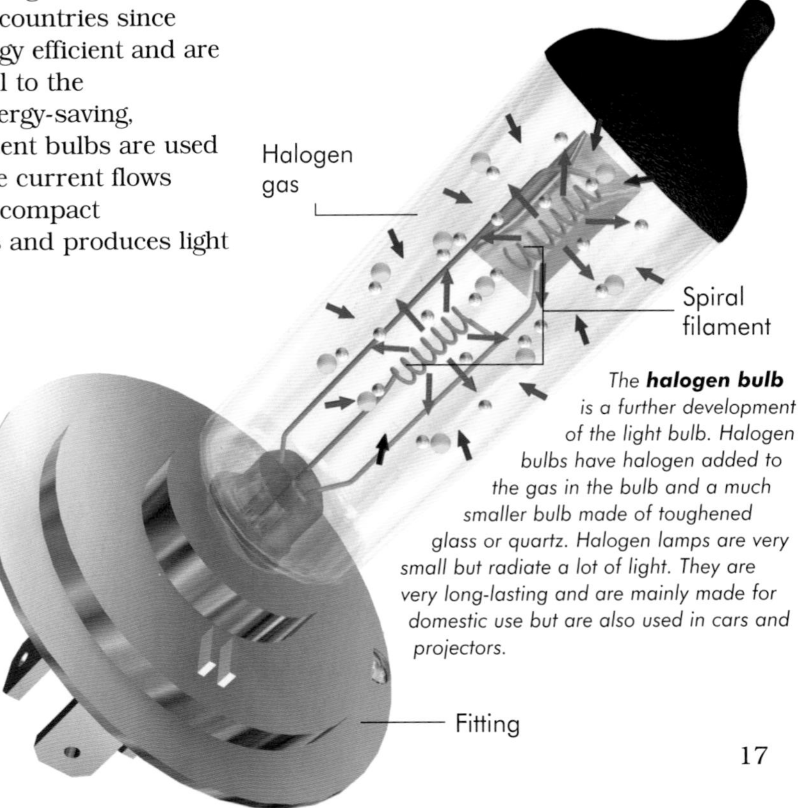

*The **halogen bulb** is a further development of the light bulb. Halogen bulbs have halogen added to the gas in the bulb and a much smaller bulb made of toughened glass or quartz. Halogen lamps are very small but radiate a lot of light. They are very long-lasting and are mainly made for domestic use but are also used in cars and projectors.*

Generators

Inspecting a generator

A generator converts kinetic energy into electrical energy. This is possible through a process known as electromagnetic induction.

Pulsating direct current

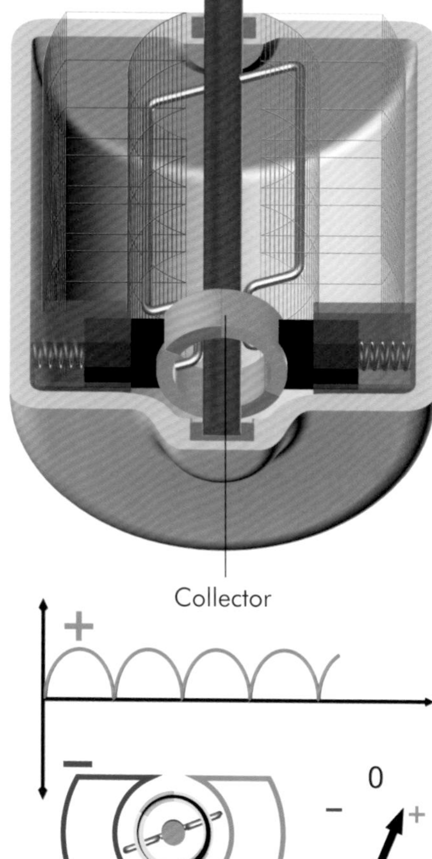

Alternating Current

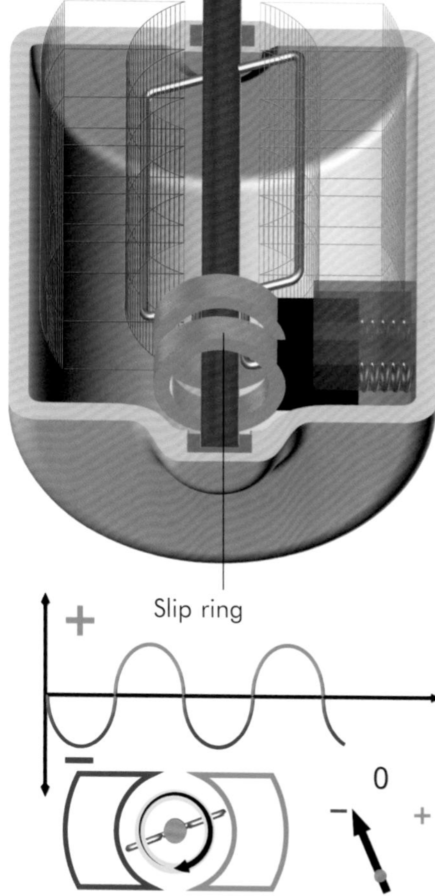

If a current is received in a 'collector', a device made up of two halves of a ring, a pulsating direct current is produced. If the current is received by two slip rings, alternating current is produced.

In 1831, Faraday (1791–1867) discovered electromagnetic induction – a process involving both electricity and magnetism. If a coil is moved around in a magnetic field an electrical current is created. However, only many years later did it become possible to create electricity for large-scale use. The invention of the electromagnetic generator in 1866, and of the direct-current generator in 1878, followed by the alternating-current generator in 1878, were all important steps in making this possible. The simplest example of a generator is a bicycle dynamo, which creates a direct current. Alternating-current generators work differently.

All generators have magnets (either permanent magnets or electromagnets) and a fixed or moveable coil. If the coil is rotated inside the magnetic field (or if an electromagnet is moved around a fixed coil), the magnetic field within the coil is altered. This means that the electrons in the coil constantly change direction, creating an alternating voltage. The strength of an alternating current depends on the rotational speed of the coil and on the strength of the magnetic field. In a direct-current generator, an alternating voltage is created first. The flow of electrons is then directed by the carbon brushes in a 'commutator' to create a direct current. This happens the moment the electrons – the current – change direction.

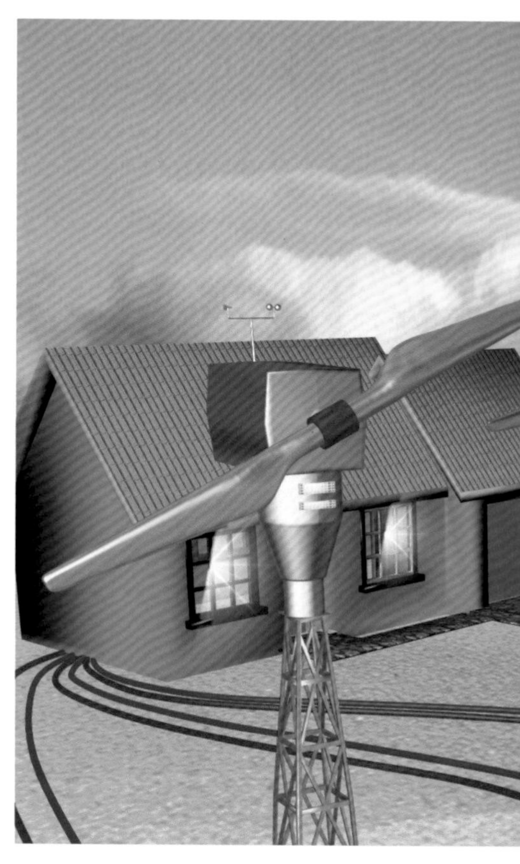

Renewable energy

Wind turbines

It is increasingly common to see wind turbines on the coast as well as on hilltops where it is usually windy. In earlier times, windmills were used to turn millstones to grind flour, or in lowland areas like Holland, they were used to pump water from low-lying sluices.

Wind turbines drive generators that deliver electricity for individual domestic use or deliver surplus electricity into a national grid. Wind energy drives generators via a gearbox, to produce several hundred Kilowatts (kW) of electricity. Wind turbines have aerodynamic rotor blades that are often placed 120 m above the ground, although a turbine can be as high as 200 m. The rotor blades can turn at speeds of up to 50 rotations a minute. Wind turbines are dependent on the changeable weather; calm periods with no wind would lead to power failure if alternative sources were unavailable. Wind farms have been erected in some coastal areas. A problem with wind farms is that they can spoil the landscape, and can also create noise pollution and be dangerous for birds.

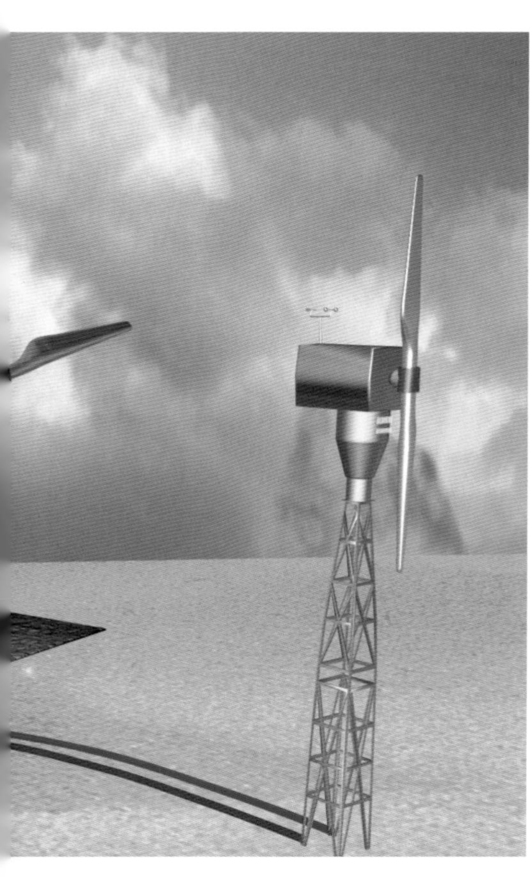

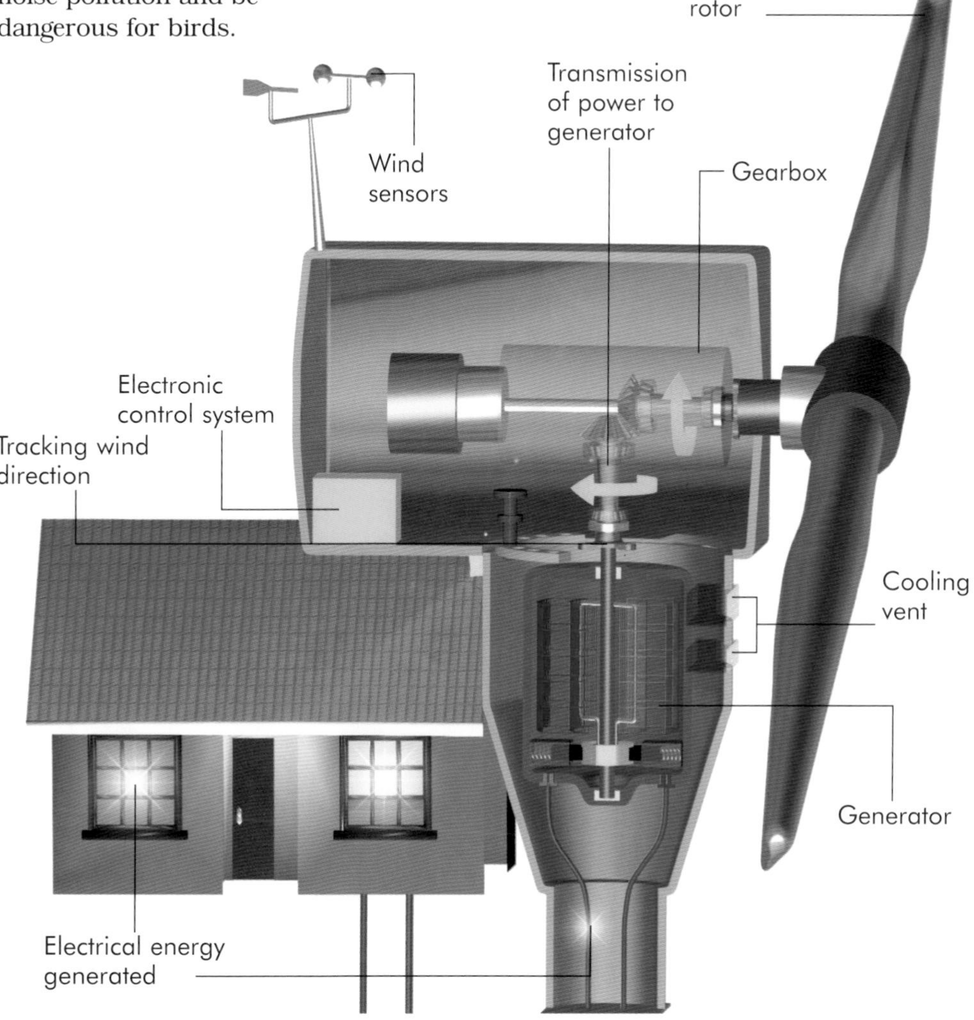

Solar cells/panels

Solar energy is an increasingly important source of renewable energy, but is a poor source of energy on days with no sunshine. A mega solar power station would require an area as big as five square kilometres covered with solar panels. In a photovoltaic system the sun's energy is converted into a direct electrical current or is used in the form of heated water for central heating systems.

Solar cells can be used instead of batteries in small gadgets and mechanisms such as calculators and watches. Experiments are being done to see if solar-powered cars and planes are possible, but they are complicated and expensive. Solar panels are often used in new housing to produce hot water and heating. Large thermal solar energy power stations that collect the sun's rays using giant mirrors have been built in places with a lot of sunshine.

Solar power station

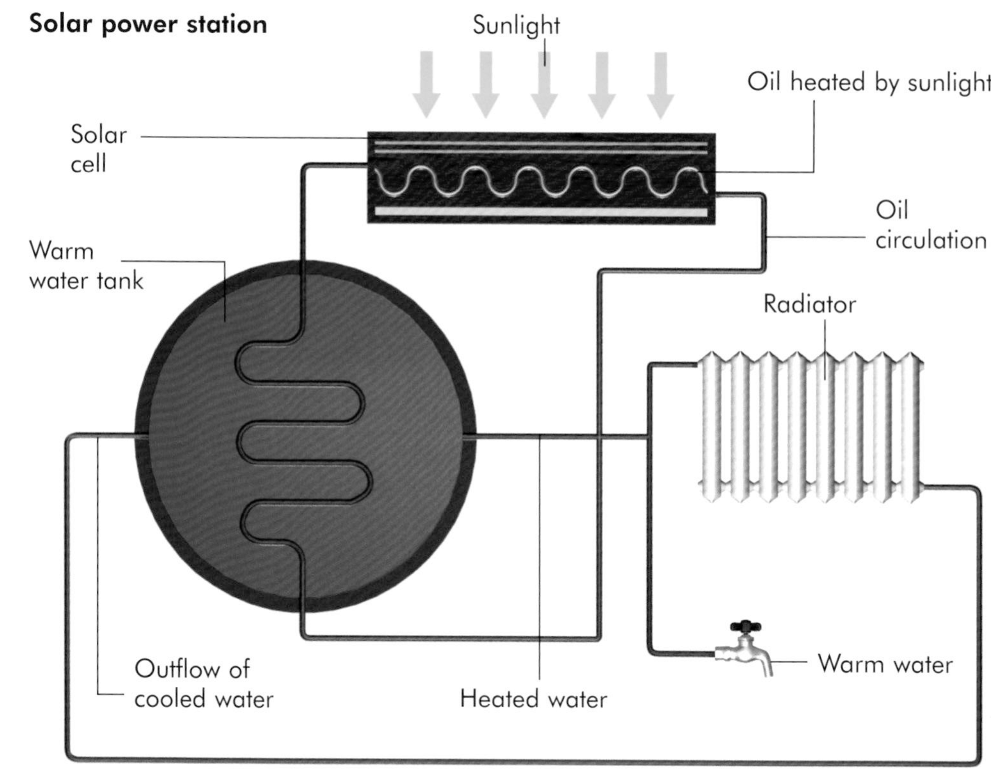

Pictures 1–3
We have recently begun to make more use of the natural energy of the sun. Solar energy is used for central heating and hot water in homes. Solar panels are placed on the roof to absorb solar energy and to heat a house via a system of pipes filled with water. The solar panels are usually flat and double-glazed in order to reduce heat loss. A flat surface below the glass absorbs the sun's rays and transmits them as heat into water pipes usually made of copper. The water is fed into radiators and taps or flows into a heat exchanger. Cold water is reheated by the solar energy collected by the panels.

Internal combustion engine

The internal combustion engine is a thermal engine driven by burning a mixture of oxygen and fuel.

Internal combustion engines are mainly used in motor vehicles. Refinements of the combustion engine are also used in ships and planes. Petrol and diesel are the most common fuels used. Gottlieb Daimler developed the petrol engine in 1883, and ten years later Rudolf Diesel invented the diesel engine, which is named after him.

In the four-stroke Otto petrol engine, named after its inventor Nikolaus August Otto, the combustion process involves four 'strokes' during which a piston moves either up or down in its cylinder four times. The strokes are: induction, compression, power and exhaust. Car engines can have 3, 4, 5 or more cylinders.

First, a fuel pump transfers fuel from a tank to the carburettor. The fuel is mixed with the oxygen needed for it to burn. Twenty parts of air are needed for one part of petrol. The combustion strokes take place inside the engine. In the first stroke, the piston moves down and sucks in the fuel and air mixture from the carburettor through an inlet valve. In the second stroke, the inlet valve closes, the piston moves up and compresses the gases, making them denser. In the third stroke, a spark created by a spark plug ignites the fuel. The expanding gases force the piston down again, generating energy. In the fourth stroke, the outlet valve opens and the exhaust gases are pushed out of the cylinder as the piston goes up, and the entire cycle can begin again.

For an engine to operate with minimal friction, the cylinder needs to be cooled and lubricated.

The camshaft, crankshaft, gearbox and transmission regulate and transmit power output.

Two-stroke engines are used in motorcycles, lawnmowers or older cars and only have compression and power strokes.

Four-stroke diesel engines need less fuel than petrol engines and, although they are more powerful, they are heavier, louder and more sluggish. They are usually used in trucks, buses, railways and ships but are also used in some cars.

In a diesel engine, the cylinder first sucks in pure air. The air is so highly compressed that it heats up to reach a high temperature of approximately 900°C. The fuel is then sprayed in the cylinder by a spray pump and ignites itself in the hot air, so no spark plugs are needed, although some diesel engines are fitted with glow plugs.

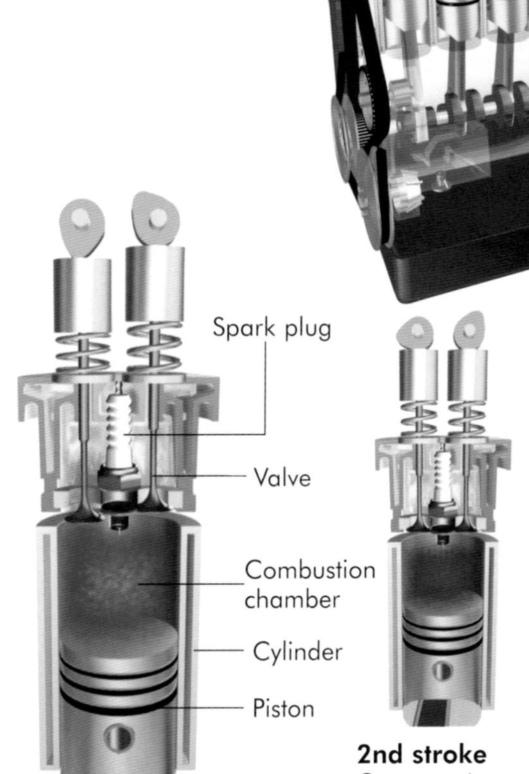

Six-cylinder petrol engine

1st stroke
Piston sucks in petrol and air mixture through an inlet.

2nd stroke
Compression stroke with closed valve (compression).

3rd stroke
Spark ignites the fuel mixture and the power stroke begins.

4th stroke
Piston pushes the exhaust gases out through the outlet valve.

Thermal power stations

In a thermal power station, thermal energy is converted to electrical energy using fossil fuels such as coal, petroleum (oil) or natural gas.

The first essential steps towards electricity generation were made with Michael Faraday's discovery of electromagnetic induction and the invention of the generator. While at one time wood was the main source of energy, today, coal, petroleum and gas are burned to create the thermal energy necessary for the production of electrical energy. The core of any power station is always the generator. In a coal-fired power station the coal is initially pulverised and burned in large boilers or furnaces. The hot gases produced in this process are channelled in a boiler with an extensive system of water-filled tubes. The hot gases heat water to produce steam at high pressure and a temperature of 500 °C. The steam then flows under high pressure into turbines connected to the generator by a drive shaft. Coal-fired power stations are often built near collieries to reduce transport costs. Power stations also use petroleum or oil. Both coal- and oil-fired power stations are damaging to the environment. Coal contains a smaller percentage of sulphur that turns into sulphur oxide during combustion and is released into the atmosphere, creating soil-contaminating acid rain. Carbon dioxide is produced whenever fossil fuels are burned, adding to the greenhouse effect.

In modern gas-fired stations, the thermal energy produced is used twice, increasing efficiency. First, gas is burned in a turbine, which drives the first of two generators. The exhaust gases produced by this process are then used to produce steam directed through other turbines to drive a second generator.

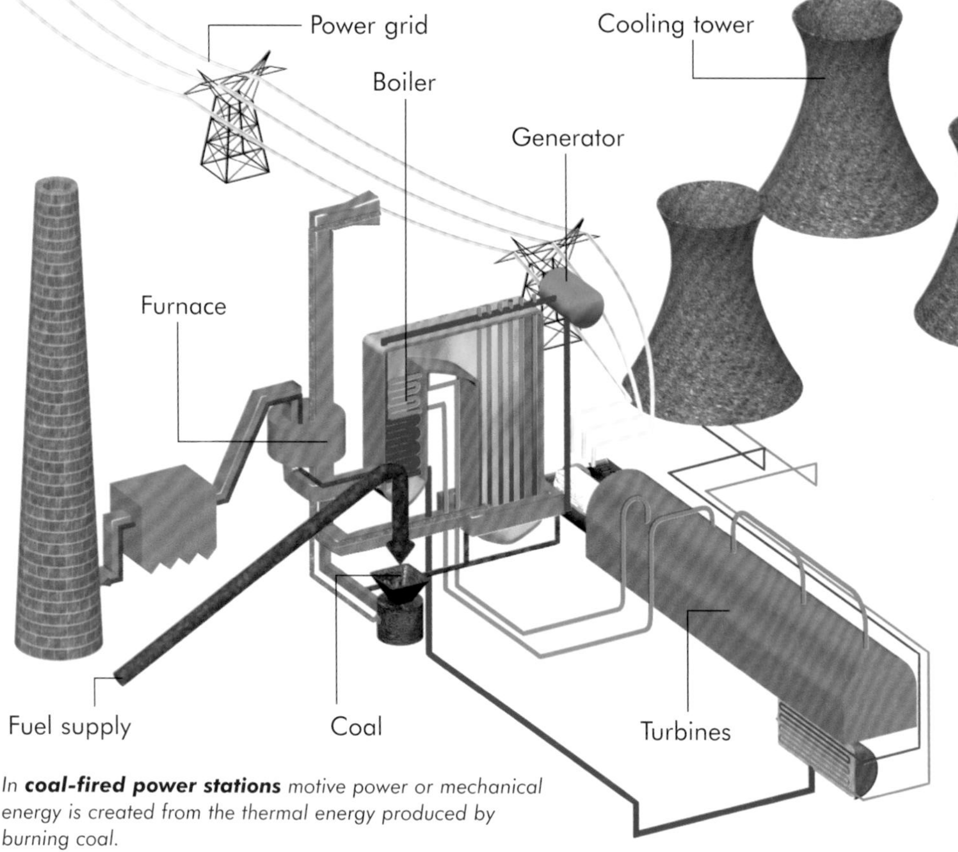

In ***coal-fired power stations*** *motive power or mechanical energy is created from the thermal energy produced by burning coal.*

Environmental damage caused by emissions
Burning coal produces environmentally damaging by-products such as carbon dioxide, which contribute to global warming and the greenhouse effect. Burning coal produces sulphur and nitrogen oxides that contribute to acid rain.

Nuclear power stations

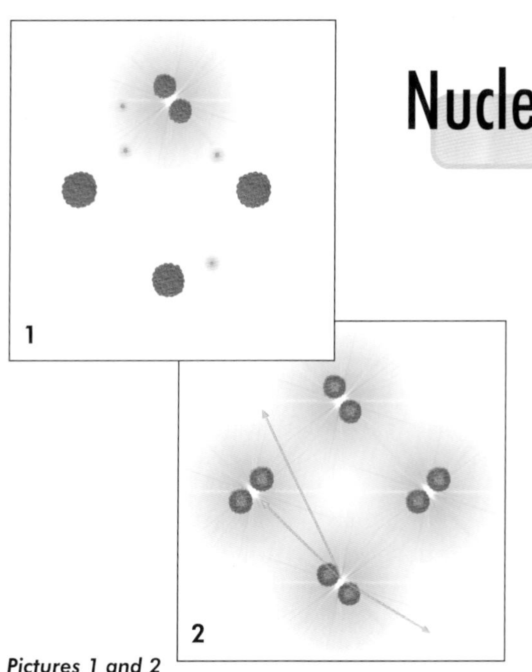

Pictures 1 and 2
In 1938 Otto Hahn and Fritz Straßmann discovered that it was possible to split uranium atoms if they bombarded them with neutrons. If Uranium 235 is struck by or reacts with a neutron it breaks apart. This process, known as 'fission', simultaneously releases energy and neutrons that then split other atoms, thereby creating a chain reaction. Unchecked, a chain reaction can go out of control and lead to a 'nuclear meltdown'.

Nuclear power stations are steam-driven stations where electrical energy is produced by splitting atoms, known as 'nuclear fission'. More energy can be produced in this way than by any other process.

The first big nuclear reactors were built in 1944 when America was looking for a way to produce plutonium to make an atom bomb. Uranium was used as fuel. The German chemist Otto Hahn had demonstrated the 'fissile' properties of uranium in 1938. In 1942, the Italian physicist Enrico Fermi succeeded in demonstrating the first nuclear chain reaction.

In order to create atomic energy in a nuclear reactor, atoms first have to be split to create a chain reaction. When the nucleus of an atom is split (uranium is the most commonly used fuel), neutrons are released and they split further atoms. To make this chain reaction possible, neutrons cannot be allowed to break free, and so the fuel used is contained in gas-tight fuel rods. The fuel rods are encased in a moderator to slow down the neutrons so that they can carry on splitting atoms. Both 'light water' (regular water) and 'heavy water' (deuterium oxide), as well as graphite, are used as moderators.

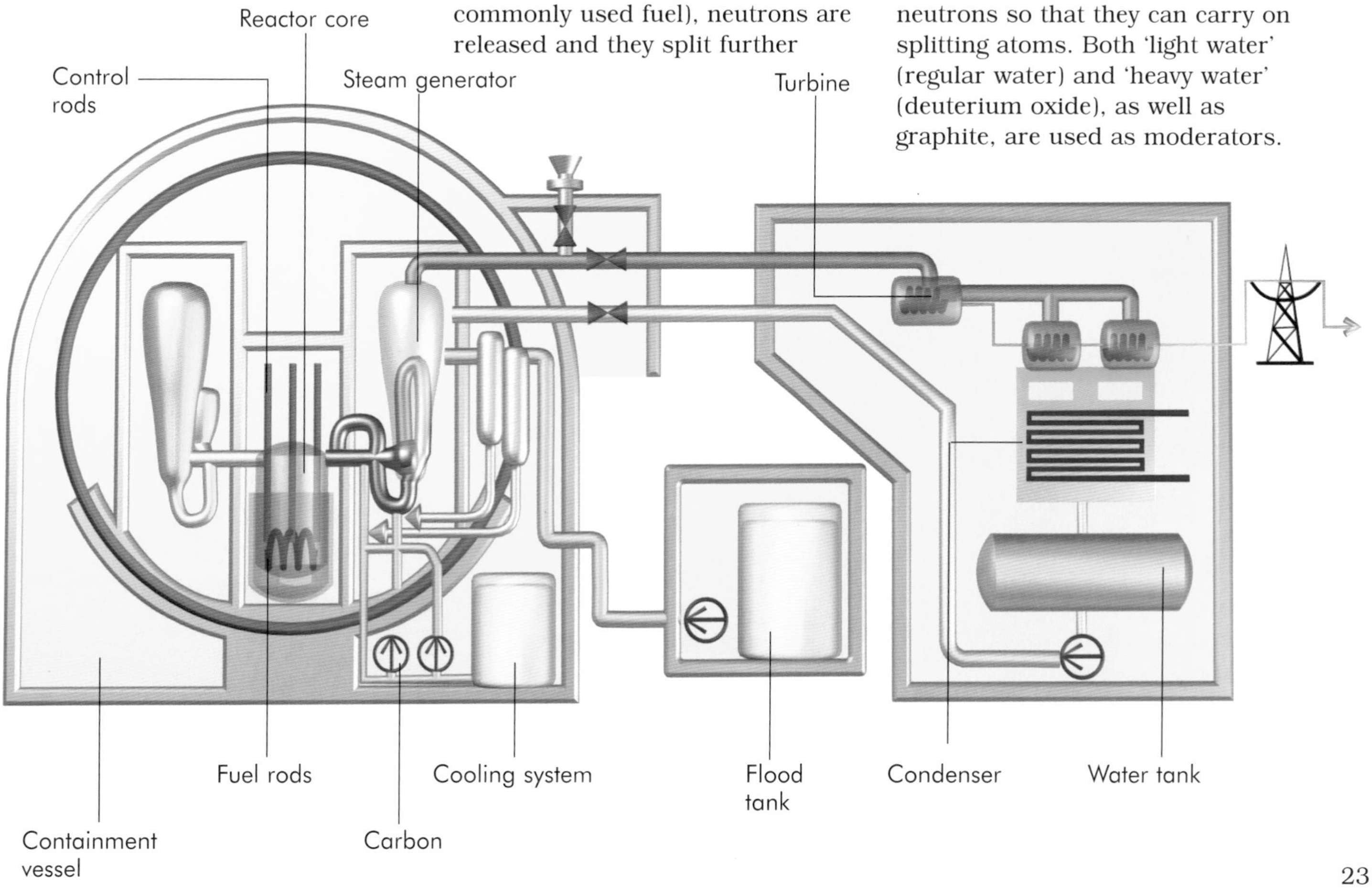

Cooling tower

Reactor core
Control rods
Steam generator
Turbine
Fuel rods
Cooling system
Flood tank
Condenser
Water tank
Containment vessel
Carbon

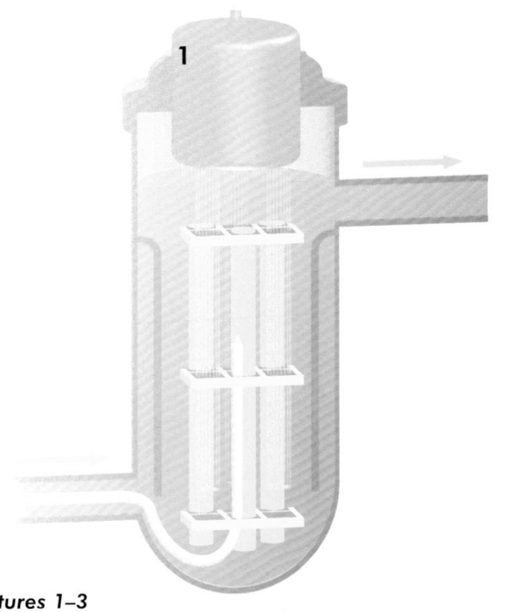

Pictures 1–3
The core of the reactor, including the fuel and control rods, is encased in a pressure vessel made of steel. A coolant circulates and absorbs the heat generated by fission. The rate of fission has to be regulated to prevent overheating and this is achieved by moving neutron-absorbing control rods in and out of the core. The heated water is turned into steam under pressure and used to drive turbines that keep a generator in operation. The generator is connected to the national grid.

To shut down a reactor, control rods can be fully inserted into the reactor. The rods absorb the neutrons and prevent further chain reactions.

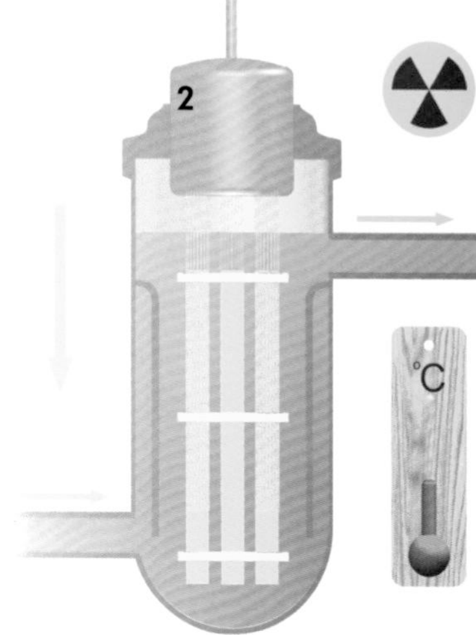

To achieve a uniformly ongoing reaction a cooling system has to be in operation near the moderator because the process of splitting atoms generates heat. The heat is discharged through a cooling system to heat water. The steam produced drives the turbines and generators. Carbon dioxide, helium, water and sodium are used as coolants. Nuclear fission produces several radioactive materials, so reactors have to be encased in various pressure and safety shields made of steel and concrete. Several other safety measures such as radiation monitors, special clothing and a safety zone around the reactor are used to ensure safety. A special reactor protection system monitors the site and alerts workers to the smallest change, while any larger variations automatically shut down the system. Nuclear reactors do not cause air pollution. However, the risks created by an accident (long-term radiation in the environment) are comparatively larger. We also have to think very carefully about how and where we dispose of the radioactive waste produced by nuclear reactors.

3

Radioactive

Operating mechanism for neutron-absorbing rods

Outflow of hot coolant

Control rods

Fuel rods of uranium dioxide in pellet form

Temperature gauge

Inflow of coolant

Pressure vessel

Hydroelectric power stations

A hydroelectric power station uses the energy from falling water to create electrical energy. Water turbines or waterwheels are used to do this.

The ancient Greeks, Romans, Chinese and Indians all knew how to put the power of water to use. The waterwheel dates back to those ancient times although it wasn't used that often since human labour was easily available and cheap. In the Middle Ages, giant waterwheels were used to drive saws and mills. Interest in the power of water grew when the turbine and generator were invented and as the demand for electricity rose. In modern hydroelectric and tidal power stations the energy of falling water is used to convert it into electricity. Water is first dammed and then directed onto turbines that turn with the gravitational force of the falling water. The turbines drive generators that convert motive power into electrical energy. The amount of energy produced depends on the height of the dam and the volume of water available. Much less power is produced by low-pressure, river-run power stations than by high-pressure stations because river weirs are very low, and the water can only be dammed up a few metres high. Raised reservoirs can be built in such cases. The collected water from a reservoir can be piped to a valley where it can drive turbines with great force. It makes sense to have tidal power stations in coastal areas where the tidal range – the difference between low and high tides – is particularly big. In estuaries or bays the range can be particularly great, even as much as ten metres or more. In tidal stations the incoming water during high tide can be dammed up and then released at low tide over turbines that drive generators to produce electricity.

No matter what progress we make in dam building or turbine technology, tidal power stations will always be expensive to build. First, the operating time of such a power station is always dependent on the tide times. Then, variations in tidal currents, silting up of the reservoirs and the effect of marine plants and animal life all create further problems. What is more, the electricity has to be moved over long distances to reach users who live far inland.

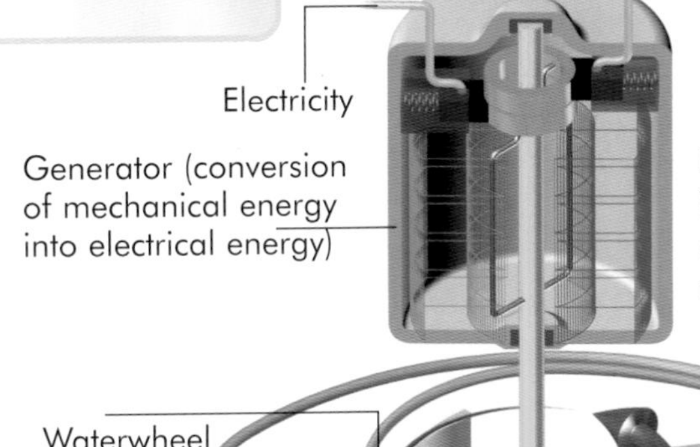

Pictures 1–3

Hydroelectric power stations are often located in mountain areas near high-lying artificial lakes – a potential source of energy. Water flowing down into the valley creates kinetic energy to drive the turbines of mills and generators. The potential energy of still water is turned into the kinetic energy of motion.
Sea vapour created by solar energy is carried in clouds from seas to high-lying artificial lakes and reservoirs and turned into potential energy. When the demand for electricity is low, electric pumps pump the water back up into the lake or reservoir to ensure sufficient water reserves during dry periods. Generators in hydroelectric stations are similar to giant dynamos.

CHAPTER 3

Land transport

People have wanted to be mobile from early on, and they have sought ways of travelling and transporting loads comfortably and without too much difficulty.

Saddles and stirrups were developed to make riding a horse, camel or donkey more comfortable. The discovery of the wheel was the beginning of the development of numerous different means of movement and transport.

First came the 'cart' that could be moved with human or animal muscle power. Wheelbarrows and other vehicles used to transport people and goods, such as carriages or 'running wheels', came next. They carried on being used, virtually unchanged, until the mid-18th century.

As early as the 17th century, several inventors tried to make use of steam power to drive vehicles. In 1770, N. J. Cugnot succeeded in travelling a short stretch at 4 km per hour with the first operative steam-powered vehicle. By 1801 a steam-powered vehicle was able to transport 10 passengers. The first steam-powered buses were used in Great Britain from 1833 onwards. Steam power was even used for two-wheelers. Today's models are not much different to motorcycles from 1900. The development of the automotive engine led to the invention of the first car in about 1885.

The railway is only about 200 years old. G. Stephenson developed the first locomotive in 1825. In 1879, the first locomotive with an electric motor was built, and trams came into existence. The first diesel-powered railway engine was built in 1925. The possibility of a magnetic railway started to be considered around 1934.

Bicycles

The '**penny-farthing**' was invented in 1870. The front wheel had a diameter of up to 2.5 m, making it a difficult bicycle to mount. It did become a popular means of transport but soon disappeared from the streets.

A bicycle is a two-wheeled means of transport propelled by pushing pedals with muscle power. The 'Draisine' or 'Dandy Horse' invented by Baron Karl Friedrich Drais von Sauerbronn is probably the most famous early bicycle. It consisted of a wooden frame with two wheels to which a seat was attached. The front wheel could be steered via the steering column. It was propelled forwards by kicking the feet off the ground. Although Drais received a patent for it for his baronetcy (Baden) it was not taken very seriously. It had a wooden frame, iron wheels, a crank drive and moveable pedals. Its description as the 'boneshaker' says it all! In the following decades, rubber or air-filled tyres, back-pedal brakes, bicycle chains and other refinements all served to improve the bicycle and to make it the most commonly manufactured mode of transport there is today. Using the same amount of energy needed for walking, considerably more distance can be covered much faster with a bicycle. Modern bicycles consist of two wheels with light metal rims, hubs with spokes and a frame made of light steel tubes. Different frames are used for bicycles for women and men.

A bicycle frame consists of a front fork connected to the handlebars, the back wheel and the pedal brackets. Brake handles are fitted on the handlebars and are connected to the wheel-rim brakes via cables. An inner tube and tyre surround the wheel rims. The back wheel is driven by chain transmission. Many bicycles are fitted with gears, making it possible to accommodate different gear ratios and maintain constant speed over variable distances. Many different types of bicycle are used for different purposes. There are city bicycles, tour bicycles, sports bicycles and mountain bicycles. Some are specially equipped and not intended for use in everyday road traffic. A recent trend is the 'e-bike', equipped with a small electric motor that is powered by a mains-rechargeable battery. The motor is activated by pedal power but can be switched off. Pedal-activated e-bikes are known as 'pedelecs'.

Shock absorbers

Disc brakes

Rim

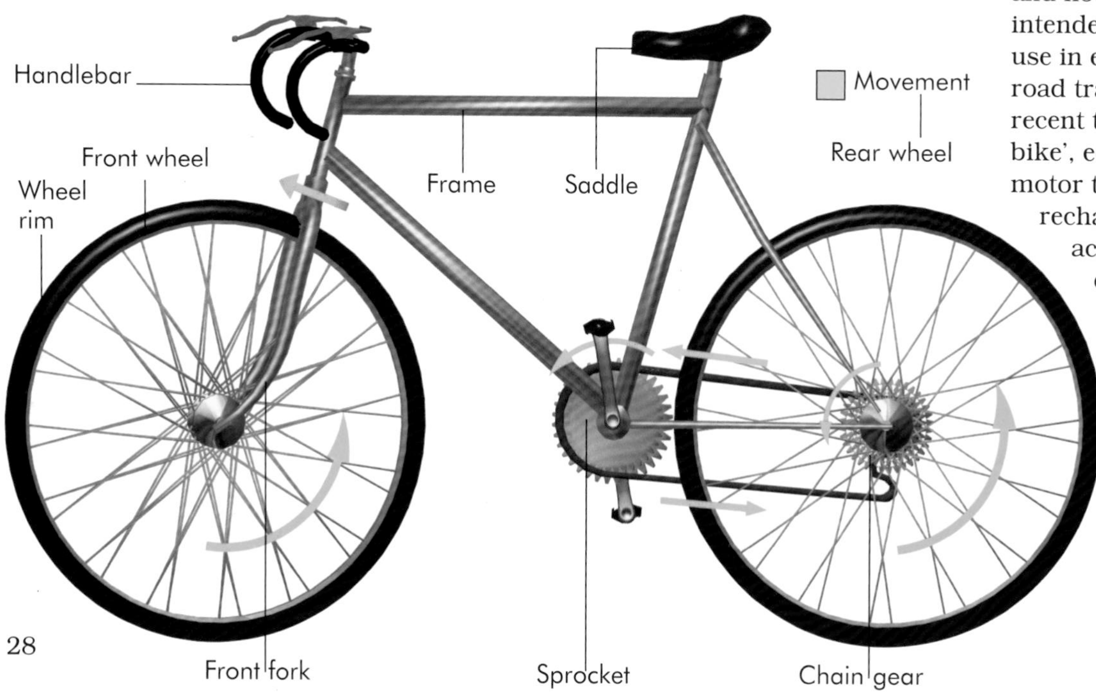

A bicycle has two spoked wheels of equal size fitted with air-filled tyres. Pedals with bottom brackets and a chain sprocket enable forward propulsion. The rear wheel is driven forward by means of a chain fitted over a small gear wheel. The pedals cover a distance of one metre with a single rotation of the chain sprocket, the rear wheel makes three rotations. A tyre with a circumference of two metres would cover a distance of six metres – six times the distance.

Motorcycles

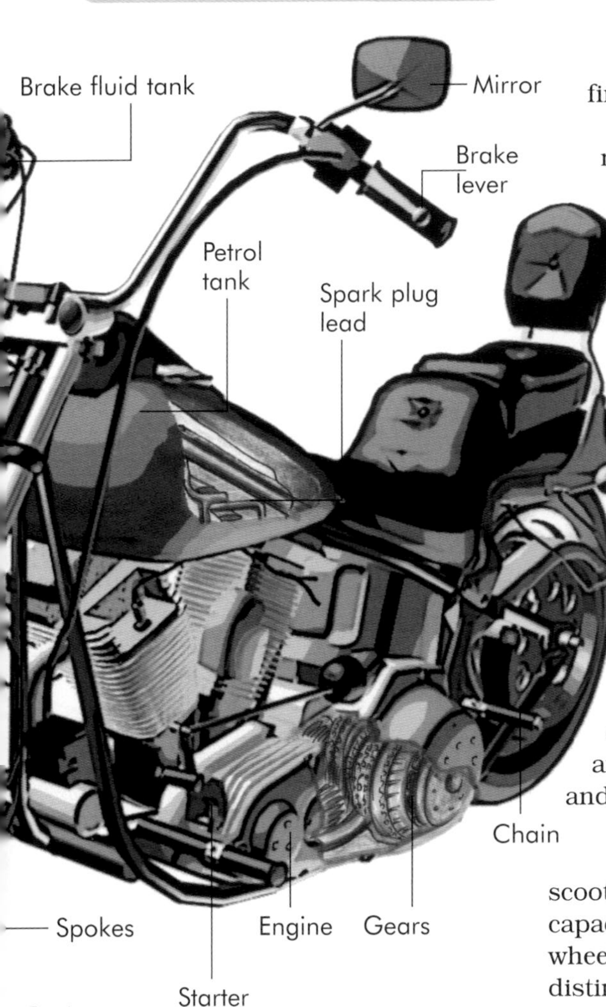

A motorcycle is a two-wheeled vehicle driven by a two- or four-stroke internal combustion engine. It is the most powerful of all two-wheelers.

The steam-powered *velocipede*, a French experiment in 1869, was the forerunner of the motorcycle. It reached speeds of 15 km per hour but was not a big success. Ten years later experiments were made with a bicycle powered by a gas-fired motor, but it soon became clear it was only possible to drive a two-wheeler with a combustion engine.

The petrol-driven 'Reitwagen' designed by Gottlieb Daimler and Wilhelm Maybach in 1885 was the first model of its kind.

The frame and wheels of the model weighing 90 kg were still made of wood. The first two-cylinder motorcycle with a four-stroke engine to roll off a production line arrived on the scene in 1894. It could reach speeds of 50 km per hour and about 1,000 models were sold.

Modern motorcycles usually have four-stroke petrol engines that are air- or water-cooled. Two-stroke engines are more common in light or sports motorcycles. A motorcycle chassis consists of wheels, suspension and frame. The clutch, gearbox and wheel drive are located between the wheels and engine. Motorcycles are classified as heavy or light motorcycles or mopeds and scooters, etc. depending on cylinder capacity, speed and power. Two-wheelers are also distinguished by their drive mechanisms: either shaft drives or chain drives, which are cheaper. In the first, torque and rotation are transmitted from the engine at the front of the cycle to the rigid rear-wheel axle via a drive shaft with two 'universal' or 'cardan' joints. Shaft-drives have the advantage of low wear and tear and need little maintenance.

Daimler's motorcycle, 1886

In a chain-drive, a chain made of articulated links transmits torque and rotation to the rear wheel. Nowadays, to prevent oil spinning off the chain at high speed, O-ring chains with seals are used. The clutch and gears are similar to those of cars.

Motorcycles vary greatly in power and comfort. Long-distance touring cycles tend to have large-capacity six-cylinder engines; road holding and power are more important in a sports motorcycle.

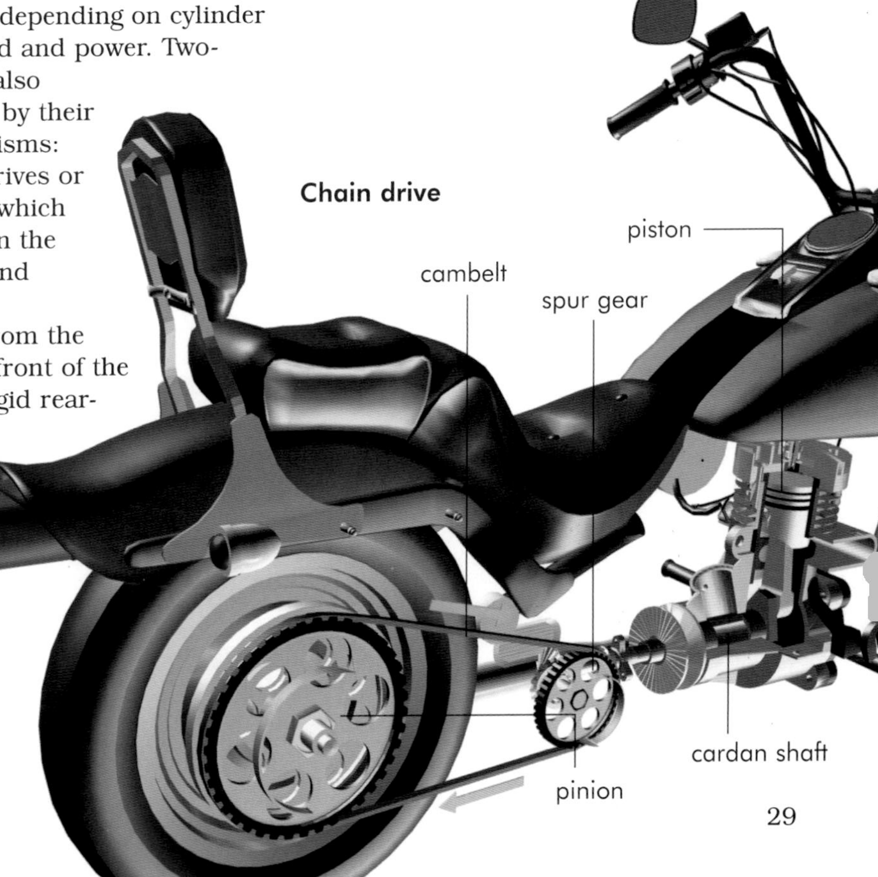

Chain drive

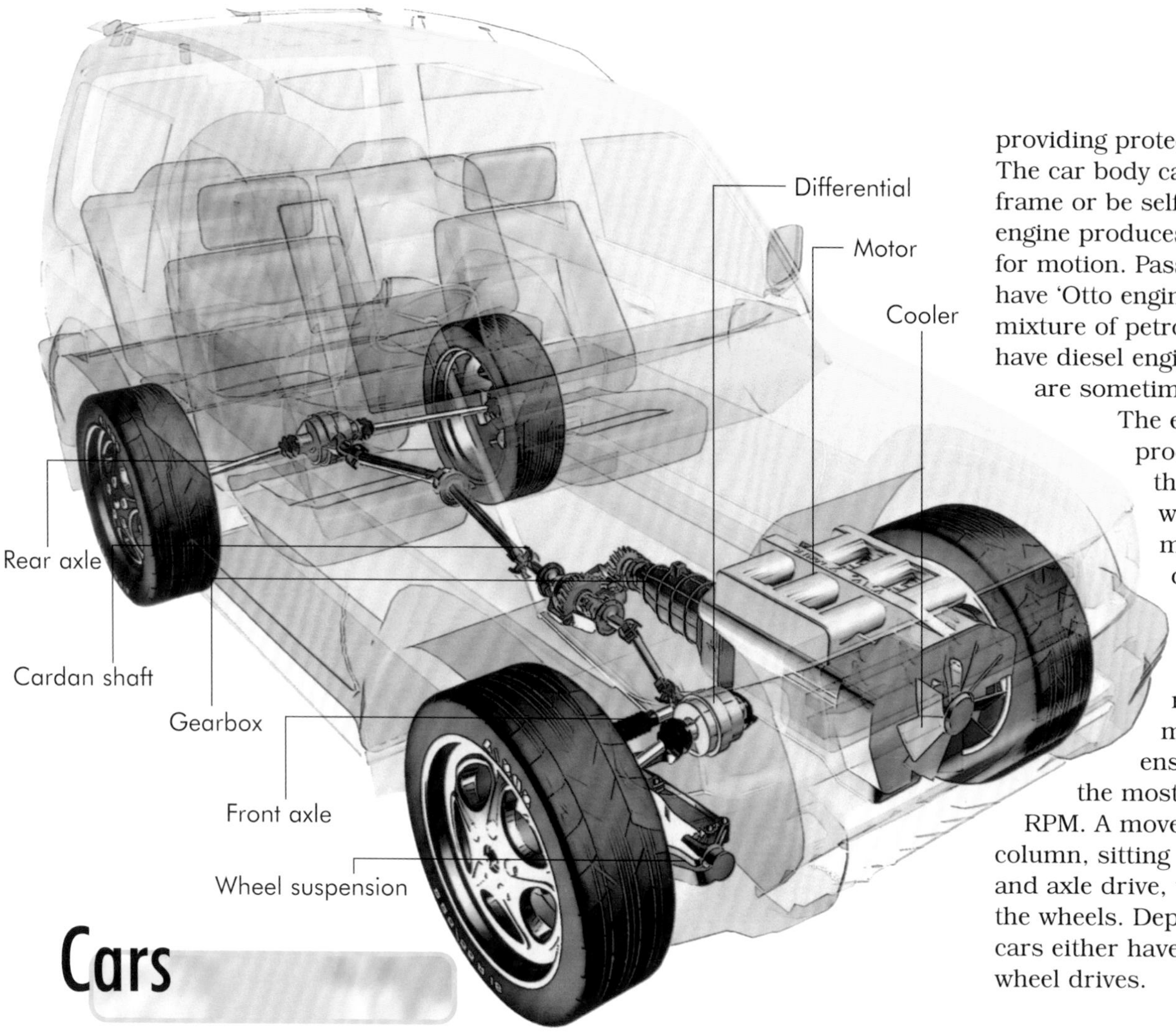

Cars

Cars are essentially vehicles for transporting people or loads. Cars have wheels with rubber tyres and are usually driven by combustion engines. Distinctions are made between passenger cars and commercial vehicles.

The Frenchman N. J. Cugnot (1725–1804) developed the first car, which was steam-powered. In 1885 C. F. Benz, a German (1844–1929) developed a four-stroke combustion engine, followed shortly by G. W. Daimler (1834–1900) and W. Maybach (1846–1929), who developed a petrol engine capable of powering a four-wheeled carriage. The elements we recognise today as usual for a car, such as air-filled tyres, exhausts and sparkplugs, were gradually added to the vehicles being developed. The first cars to roll off an assembly line were manufactured by Ford Motors in 1913.

Assembly line, 1930

Every car has three main elements:

1. The chassis holds the engine and consists of the wheels and tyres, car frame, springs, suspension, shock absorbers, steering and brakes. 2. The car body sits over the frame, gives a car it's shape and shields passengers from the cold, noise and the airflow produced during driving, as well providing protection in an accident. The car body can either sit on the frame or be self-supporting. 3. The engine produces the power needed for motion. Passenger cars usually have 'Otto engines' driven by a fuel mixture of petrol and air or they have diesel engines. Electric motors are sometimes used.

The engine burns fuel to produce energy that is then transmitted to the wheels by various means. The clutch connects the gears to the crankshaft, which adjusts the engine's torque and revolutions per minute (RPM) to ensure the car moves at the most efficient rate of RPM. A moveable steering column, sitting between the gears and axle drive, transmits power to the wheels. Depending on the model, cars either have rear-, front- or four-wheel drives.

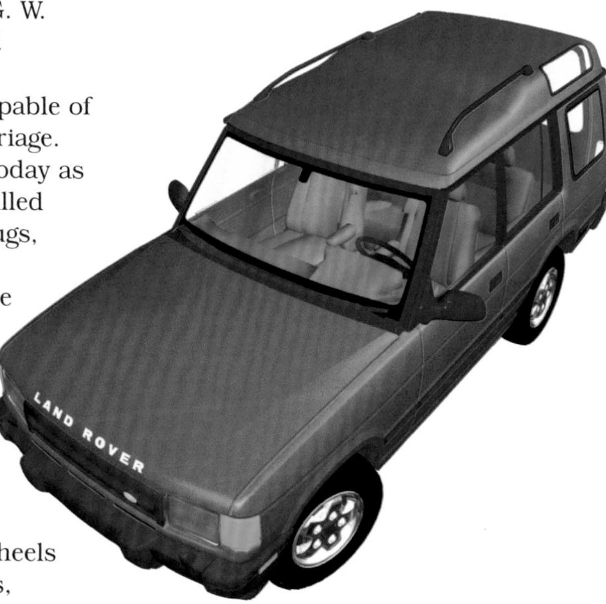

Lorries

Lorries are engine-powered commercial vehicles used for transporting goods or loads, depending on the type of lorry.

The first lorry was a large steam-powered cart developed by N. J. Cugnot in 1771. In 1825 steam-powered tractors and buses were developed and in 1896 G. Daimler and W. Maybach pioneered the development of a lorry with a petrol engine. Initially, it resembled a self-propelled horse carriage and moved very slowly (at approximately 2 km per hour). Thirty years later, lorries with diesel engines and different kinds of body, such as boxes, flatbeds and tippers, started to be developed. Lorries are classified into different groups depending on a number of features. For example, light, medium and heavy lorries are classified according to their load-carrying capacity. Trailers are another kind of lorry, including articulated lorries and semi-trailers. A semi-trailer is connected to a lorry with steel pivots and bars and is detachable. It doesn't have a front axle, and is instead stabilised with retractable legs. Lorries have cabins or 'cabs' for the driver. The cab is either 'conventional', where the engine has a long bonnet and is in front of the cabin, or 'cab-over', where the engine is either behind or under the cab. In many lorries the cab can be tipped over when repairs are needed.

In articulated lorries with trailers, the coupling and connecting rods are located at the rear above the front axle of the trailer. An in-built 'bogie' makes it possible to drive around bends. In some models, the distance between the lorry and the trailer is controlled by means of a hydraulic rod.

The number of axles or wheels is another feature used to differentiate lorries. Road traffic regulations determine the width, height and length of lorries. Driving times, how long a lorry driver can drive for and rest periods are all regulated as well, and 'tachographs' installed in the driver cabins keep track of these things. Modern lorries usually have diesel engines and automatic transmission with up to 16 gears. A Class C driving license is needed to drive a lorry with a total weight of 7.5 tonnes.

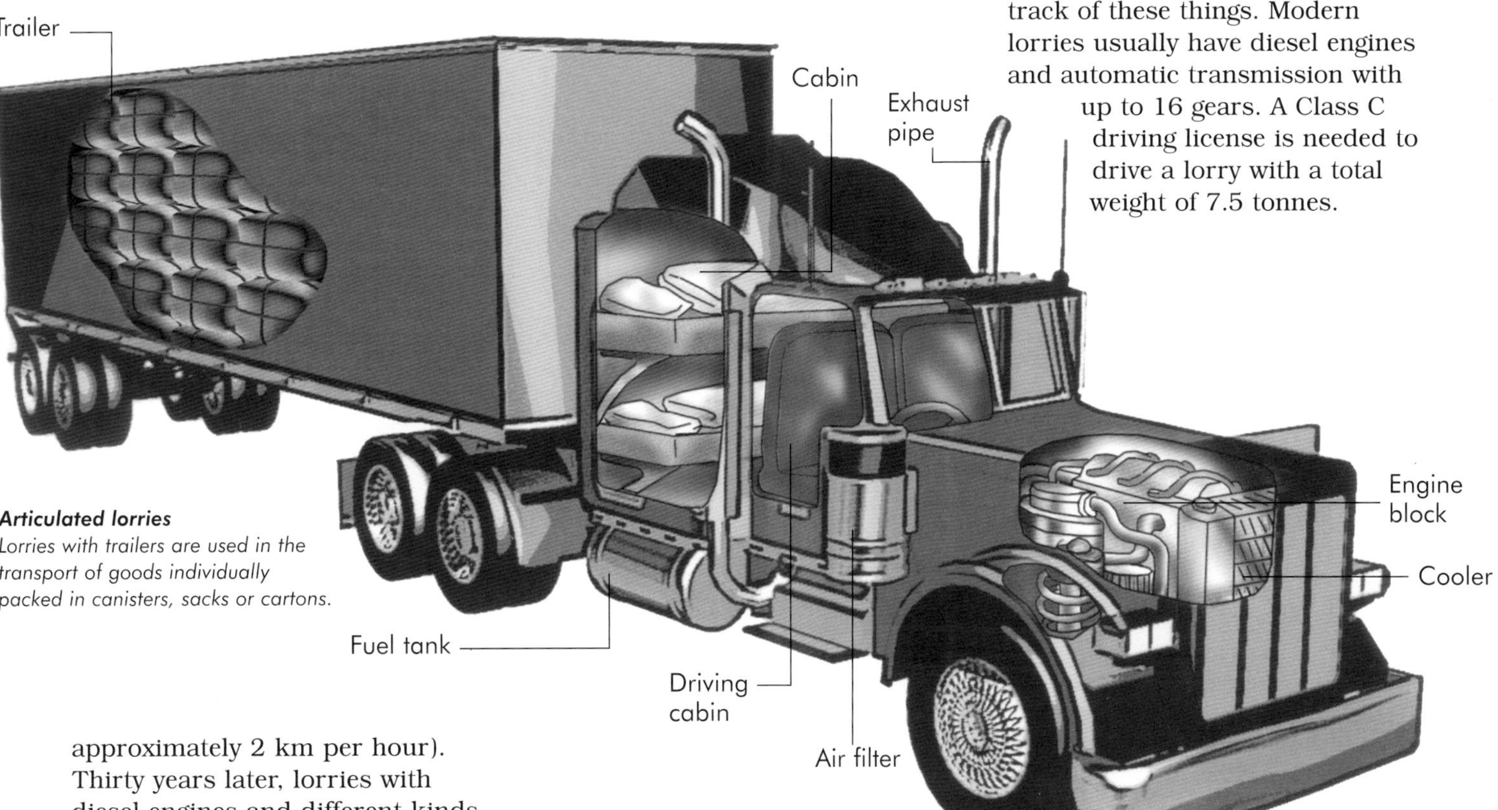

Articulated lorries
Lorries with trailers are used in the transport of goods individually packed in canisters, sacks or cartons.

Railways

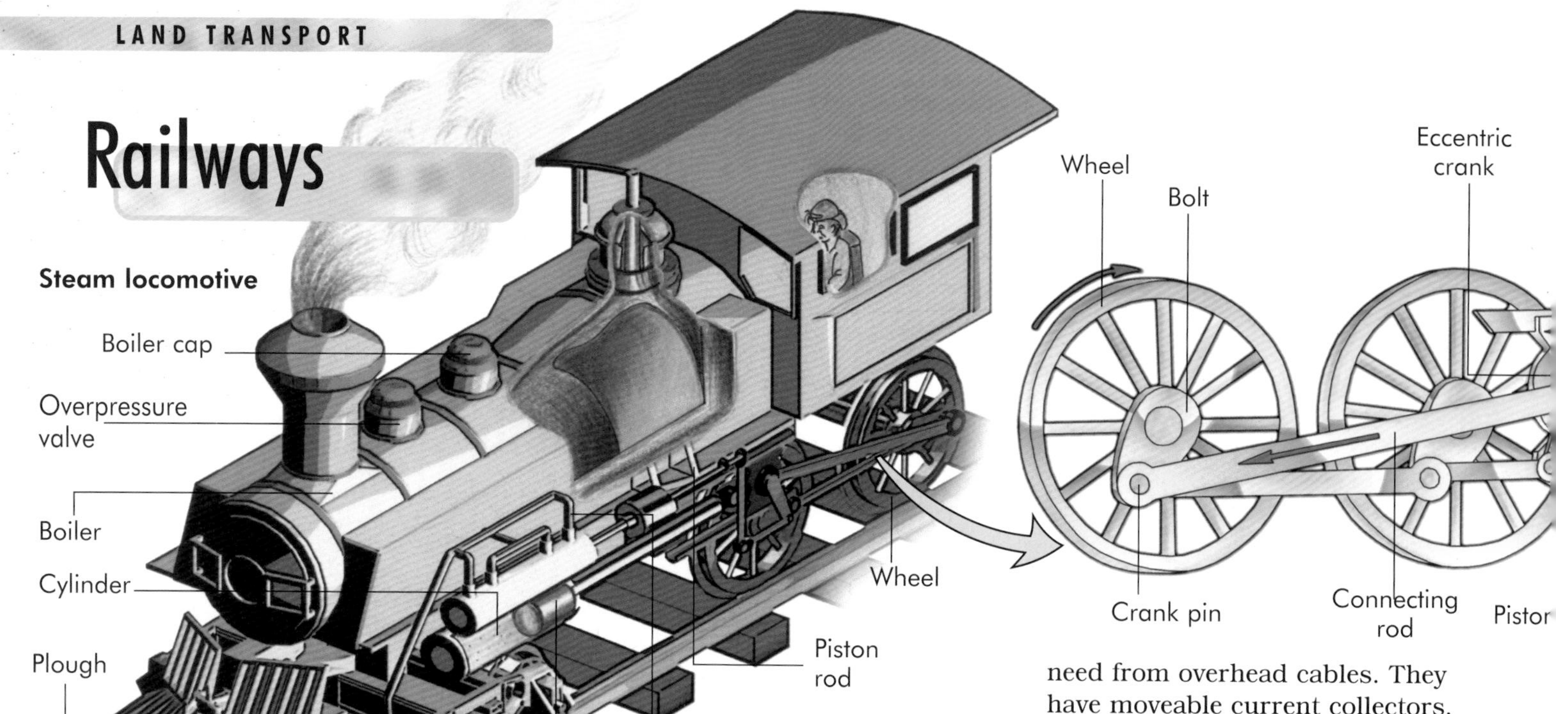

Railways are a way of transporting people or goods in trains that run on rails. Trains are pulled or pushed by railway engines with different types of combustion engine. The first railway trains were horse-drawn. Steam trains began to be built from 1803 onwards. One of the first and most famous was R. Trevithick's 'Catch-me-as-you-can'. The first railway line for public transport was authorised in 1825 and was 39 km long. The 'Rocket', built by George Stephenson, was the model for later versions of railway engine, and in 1829 he built a railway line from Liverpool to Manchester.

Steam trains were kings of the railway for nearly 100 years but have long since been replaced by electric and diesel locomotives. The last steam engine to be used in the UK made its final journey in 1968. They are still in use in some countries, such as China, for example. The first electric engine was used in the USA in 1884 and in Germany in 1911.

Electric engines have to carry their source of power with them. They usually get the electricity they need from overhead cables. They have moveable current collectors, which are always connected to the overhead cables and the engines draw electric current through them. Overhead cables usually receive an alternating current, which is converted into direct current in the railway engine. Some systems use live rails instead, but they are more expensive to install. Some energy-saving engines even have systems where the heat generated by braking is converted into electrical current and stored in the overhead-cable system.

Overhead cables are expensive to install and they are only used where many trains, especially passenger trains, are in operation. Diesel engines are classified according to whether a diesel-hydraulic or diesel-

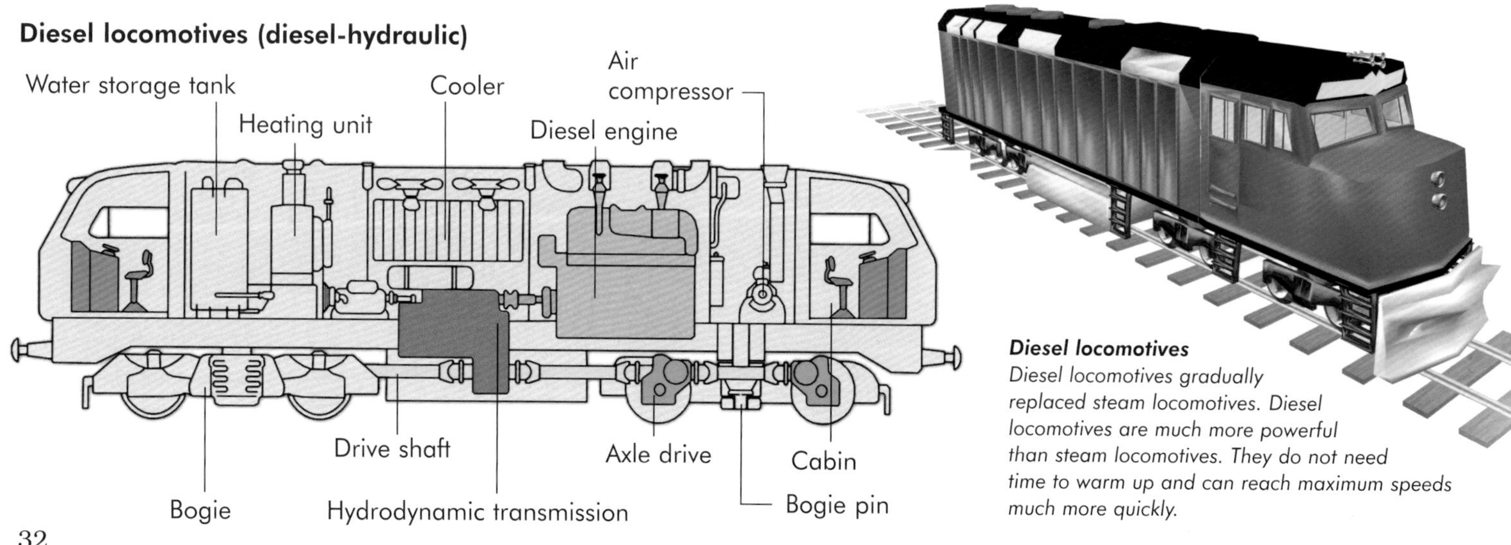

Diesel locomotives
Diesel locomotives gradually replaced steam locomotives. Diesel locomotives are much more powerful than steam locomotives. They do not need time to warm up and can reach maximum speeds much more quickly.

electric system is used. Diesel-hydraulic systems are less common. In this system, a hydraulic clutch and gearbox adjust the speed of revolutions between the engine and wheels. In a diesel-electric a generator is driven by a diesel engine, to provide the current for the electric motor.

In 1991, in Germany, High Speed Trains (the Intercity Express or ICE) were introduced for regular service. They have maximum speeds of over 300 km per hour, are equipped with special suspension systems, passenger information systems including screen displays and telephones, for example, and have very comfortable seating. Since it is expensive to lay and maintain new railway lines and tracks, the ICE trains only run where there is high passenger demand.

Electric locomotive

Electric locomotive

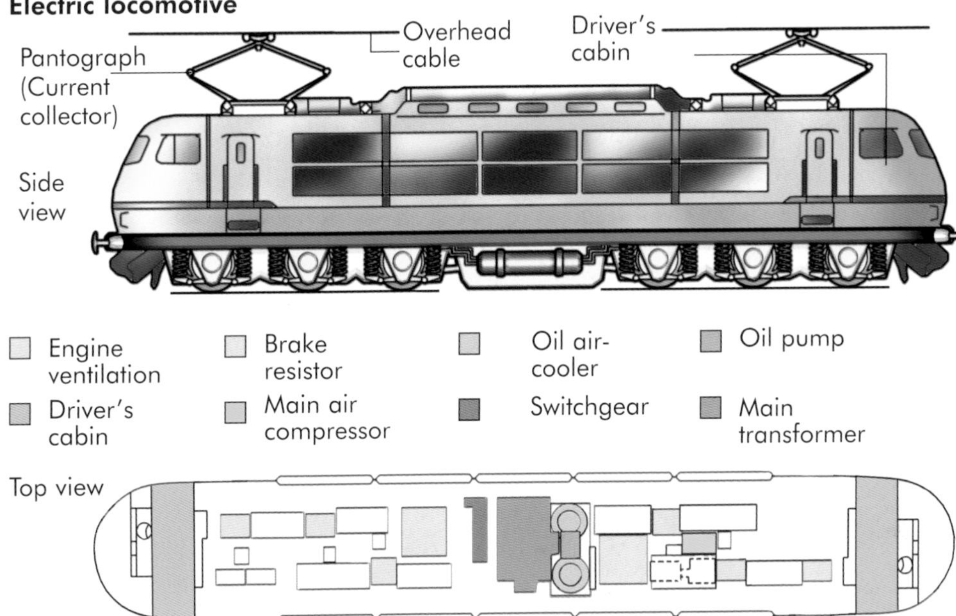

Monorails

Monorails are railway systems that only use a single rail. Monorail suspension systems were in use as early as 1821.

There are two basic types of monorail: straddle-beam and suspended. In a straddle-beam monorail the railcars straddle a track with a driving mechanism. Additional drive wheels stabilise the cars on the track. By contrast, a suspended monorail, such as the one built in 1900 by Wuppertaler Schwebebahn, hangs below the track.

The Maglev (short for Magnetic Levitation) monorail is one of the most modern versions of monorail. The Maglev trains use either an electrodynamic or an electromagnetic system. The Transrapid trains developed in Germany use the electromagnetic system and can reach speeds of up to 500 km per hour.

Levitation magnets below the train suspend it above the track, while guidance magnets on the side guide the train along the track. Linear induction motors drive the trains. The motors are flat, unlike normal electric motors, enabling them to constantly create a moving electromagnetic field, which propels the train.

Electromagnetic suspension monorail (EMS)

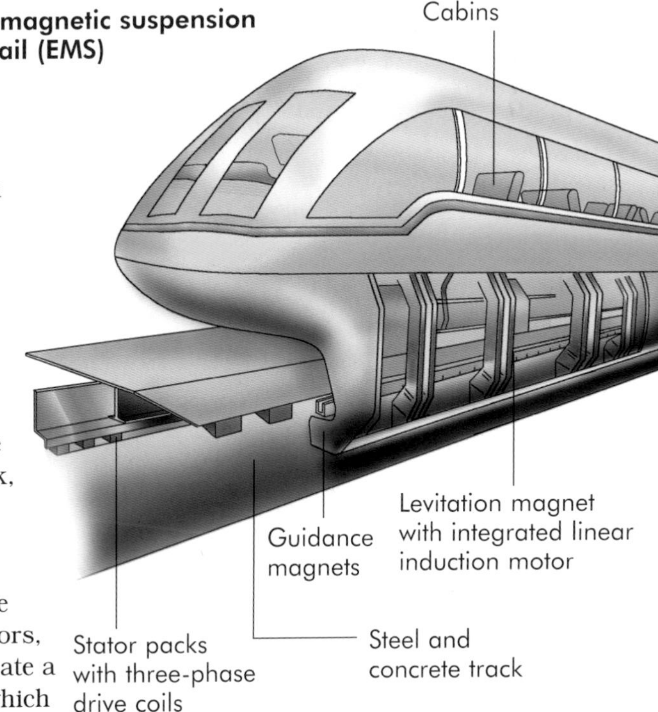

CHAPTER 4

Air transport

People have always dreamed of flying. We've probably all heard the Greek myth of Icarus, who tried to fly using wings made of bird feathers. Leonardo da Vinci is also famous for his sketches of parachutes and flying machines but he never succeeded in making them work. The Montgolfier brothers were the first to succeed in flying – in a hot-air balloon – in the 18th century.

Airships were the first mode of flight that could be steered, and in 1891 Otto Lilienthal, making use of rising air currents, became the first man to fly a glider. The Wright brothers, Orville and Wilbur, built the first powered aircraft in 1903. The development of increasingly powerful engines eventually made it possible to expand air traffic into the worldwide network of airlines we have today.

The helicopter, which could rise and land vertically, was another new development at the beginning of the 20th century.

To achieve higher speeds, physicists and inventors considered using rocket power for aircraft. This principle had already been used in fireworks in China as far back as the 13th century, and since the 18th century rockets had been used for signalling, mainly by the military, but also in whaling. It was only at the end of the 19th century that scientists began using rockets for the exploration of outer space. The first successful attempt was in 1957 with the 'Sputnik' satellite. It orbited the earth at a speed of 28,000 km per hour. The first person to travel into outer space was followed by the first Moon landing. Space shuttles transport several probes into outer space to bring us the latest news and weather reports as well as images and measurements of other galaxies both far and near to ours.

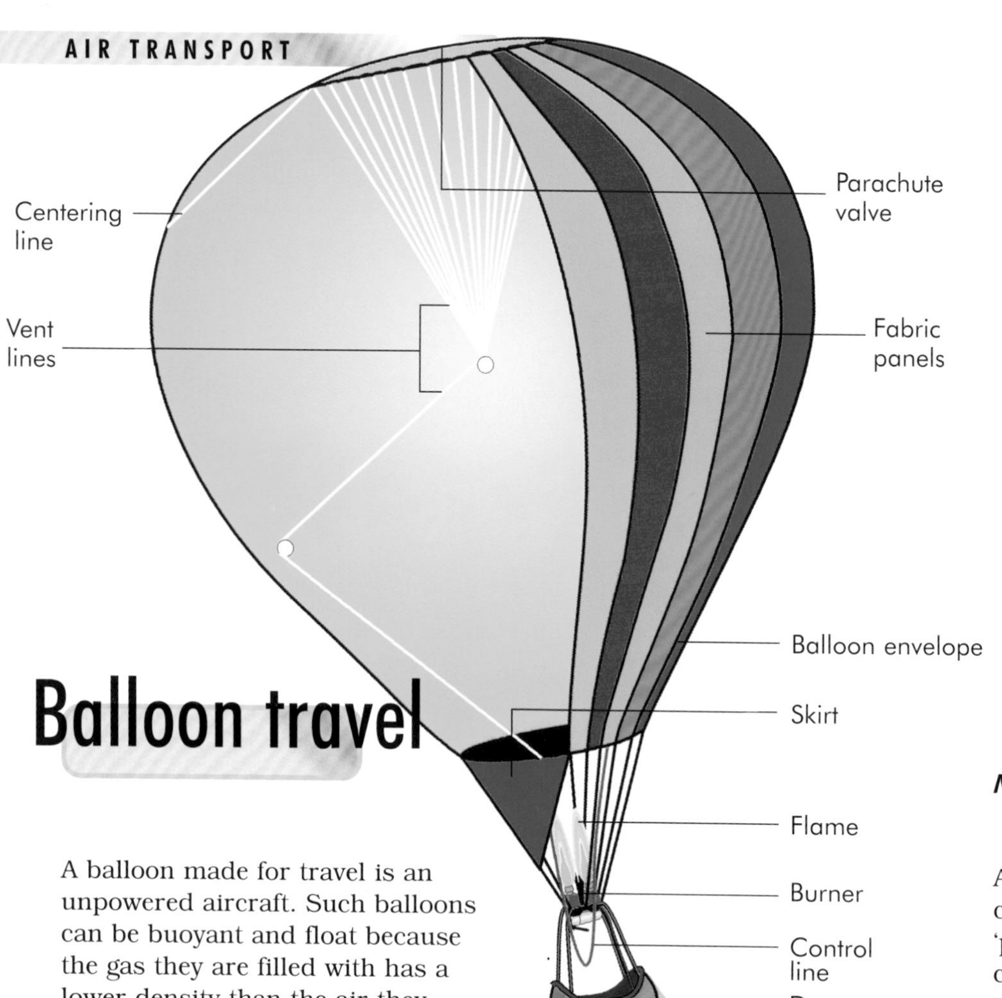

Balloon travel

A balloon made for travel is an unpowered aircraft. Such balloons can be buoyant and float because the gas they are filled with has a lower density than the air they displace.

In 1783 the brothers J. E. and J. M. Montgolfier released a balloon filled with hot air. They are credited with being the inventors of balloon travel althought the first attempts were in fact made in China in 1300. In 1783 the first hydrogen-filled balloon was also released. It stayed aloft for two hours. Another balloon, called the 'Charlière', after it's inventor J. A. C. Charles, had a greater load-bearing capacity than the 'Mongolfière'. To this day balloon travel has been undertaken using balloons based on these two types of balloon.

The Montgolfière over Paris
In 1783 the Marquis d'Arlandes and Pilatre de Rozier floated above Paris in a colourful hot air balloon made by the Montgolfier brothers.

Hot-air balloons used for sport and leisure are very similar to the first models. The balloon envelope is made up of several panels of fabric that are sewn together, with an opening at the bottom. The air inside the balloon is heated through the opening by a propane gas burner. The gas burner sits below the opening, in a basket, and is protected by a special sail (the balloon 'skirt'). When the air inside the balloon envelope has been heated sufficiently, it begins to rise.

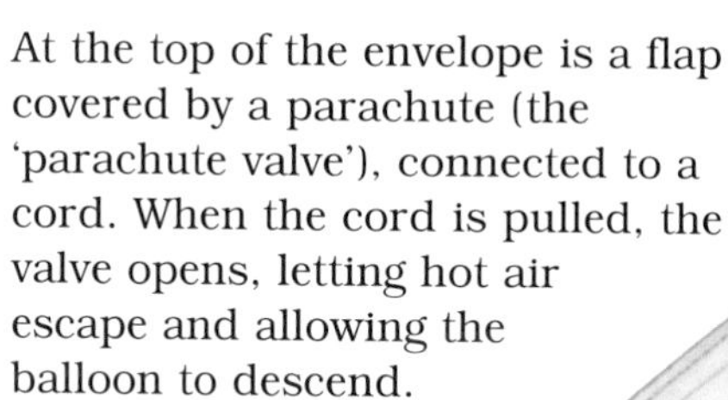

Montgolfière

At the top of the envelope is a flap covered by a parachute (the 'parachute valve'), connected to a cord. When the cord is pulled, the valve opens, letting hot air escape and allowing the balloon to descend.

Gas balloons work somewhat differently. They are made of closed envelopes filled with helium or hydrogen. A basket for passengers or ballast hangs below the balloon, attached to a net that encases the envelope. The ballast, usually sacks filled with sand, has to be thrown out of the basket to allow the balloon to rise. A valve has to be opened to allow the balloon to descend. As the gas escapes, buoyancy diminishes and the balloon sinks. Shortly before landing, a 'rip panel' is opened by a cord, allowing the remaining gas to escape quickly to avoid the balloon being dragged across the ground for too long.

Airships

Airships are streamlined balloons filled with a light gas. They are self-propelled with a propeller and rudder.

After the first successful balloon rides, the aim was to try and travel in balloons to get to particular places. This would involve a means of powering a balloon in order to steer it. Several experiments with hand-operated rudders followed, steam power was considered and even the use of trained eagles! The first usable airship was an invention of Count F. Zeppelin, who flew the first rigid ship in 1900. It was propelled by two 15 horsepower Daimler engines and reached speeds of 32 km per hour. The Zeppelin took passengers a few years later.

A modern Zeppelin has a streamlined body with a rigid metal frame covered with a fabric envelope. Individual chambers at the bottom are filled with hydrogen or helium. Passengers and crew sit in a gondola hanging from the underbelly of the ship's envelope. A second gondola houses the engines and propellers. At the back of the Zeppelin are the tailfins and rudders. In 1937, in a terrible accident in Lakehurst, USA, a Zeppelin known as the *Hindenburg* exploded. Thirty-five people, including passengers and crew, died in the accident, and it put an end to any further development of airships.

In contrast to rigid airships, semi-rigid airships are often used today for advertising or pleasure trips. They also have a cigar-like shape when filled, but have no metal frame. A gondola for passengers and engines hangs below the body of the ship. Semi-rigid airships are too loud to carry passengers, however, and are difficult to navigate.

***Zeppelin* Airship in London, 1931**

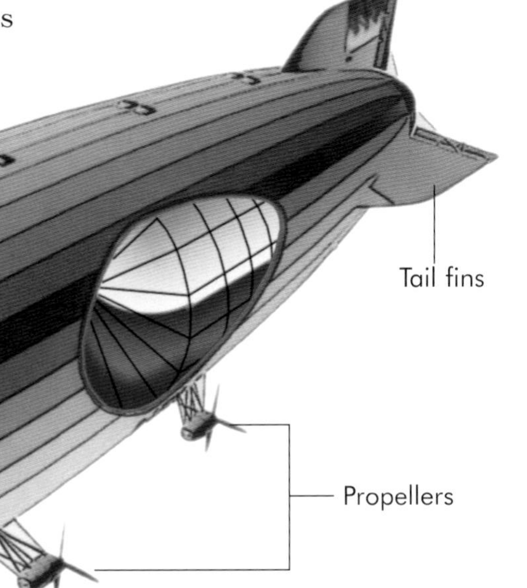

Building an airship
Rigid airships had a rigid frame of metal or wood and a cotton envelope. Inside the frame, individual airtight chambers were filled with hydrogen.

Gliders

Long wings

Streamlined cockpit

Rudders for horizontal movement

Smooth fuselage for reduced air resistance

Ailerons for tilting when flying in a curve

Elevators for vertical movement

Gliders are unpowered aircraft supported in flight by updraughts.

As far back as 1891, Otto Lilienthal made several flights in a glider. Unfortunately he later died in an accident. A few years after Lilienthal, before they became famous for flying powered aircraft, the Wright brothers also experimented with gliding. In 1922, hour-long flying competitions were held over the mountain of Wasserkuppe in the Rhön region of Germany. Until the Second World War this was the centre of gliding as a sport. Before a glider can take flight it has to be pulled by a powered towing aeroplane or a rope winch has to be used in order to launch it in the air. The wings then provide the lift that it needs. Just like other planes, the curved shape of the topside of the wing (known as an aerofoil) makes this possible. The curve of the wing means the air passing above the wing covers a larger area than the air passing below, creating a difference in pressure. The wings are also relatively long, which means that air above the wing will also flows inward and air flowing below will flow outward. Small eddies forming at the wing tips act like brakes, although using narrower wings can reduce this effect.

A glider's 'lift' increases in conjunction with its speed, but speed also increases wind resistance, which has a braking effect. In order to fly faster a glider has to first fly downward. A glider can fly longer and further by making use of air currents. Upward air currents are created above heated ground or in built-up areas. If a glider flies in such rising air it will go higher.

Unlike unpowered gliders, some gliders are fitted with small motors on the plane's tail. The motor can't be used to launch the glider, but it helps to maintain height where there are no up-draughts. Gliders with motors are as light as motorless gliders and have the same wing shape.

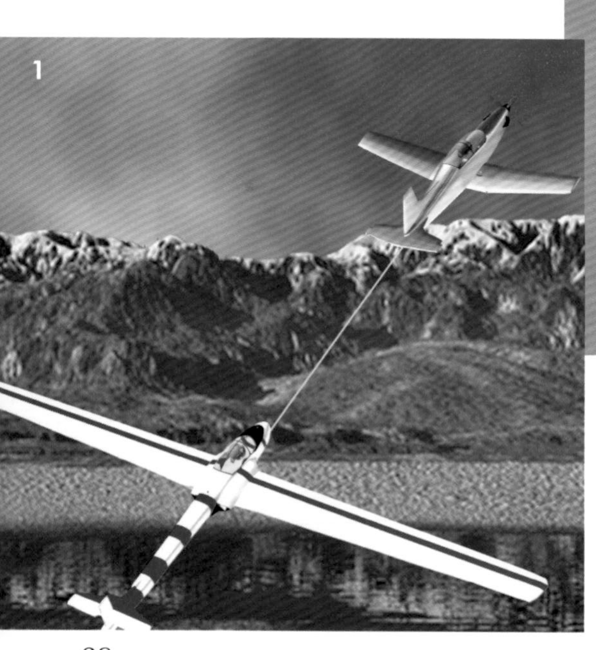

2

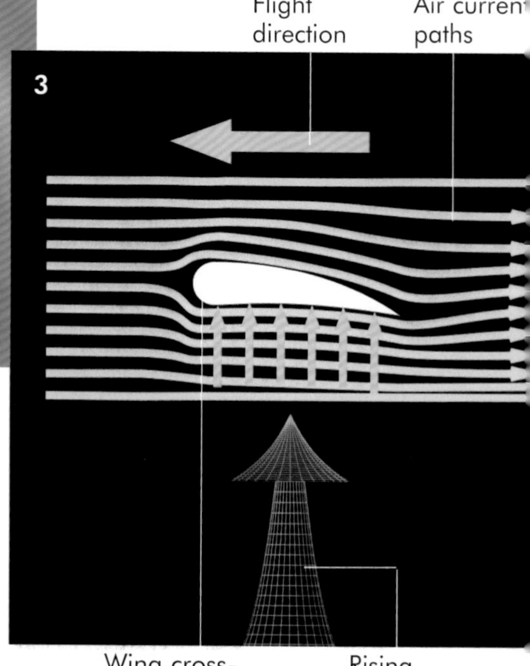

Pictures 1–3
Gliders are made of light materials such as glass fibre. Thermals and forward movement are used to launch a glider. By using information about the weather and ground conditions a pilot can get a glider to rise. Extensive flights are possible if the craft climbs high enough.

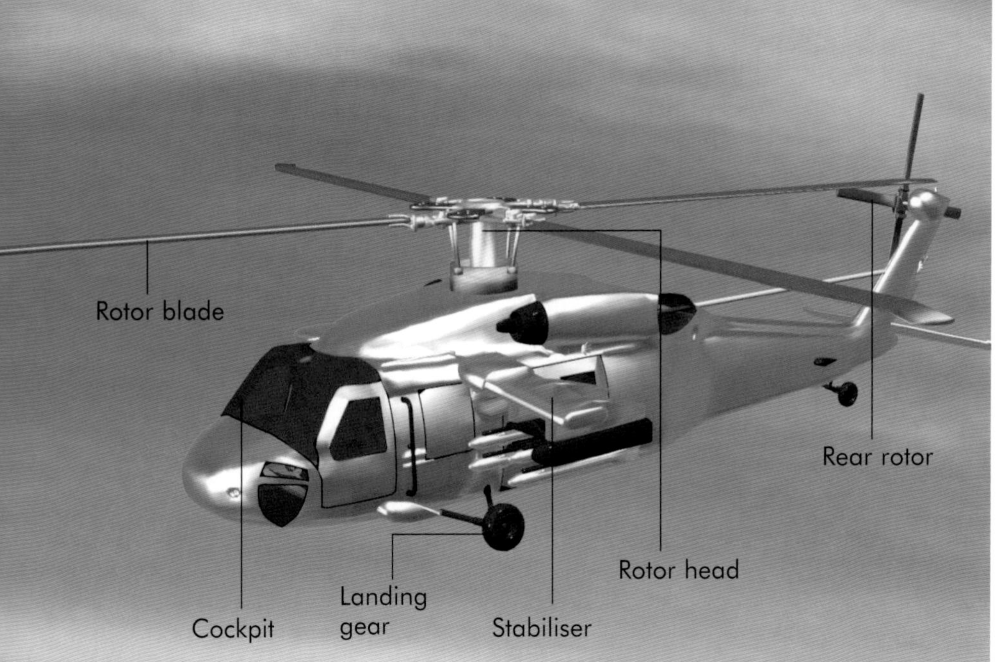

Pictures 1–3
A pilot can set the helicopter's enormous rotor blades at different angles to force the helicopter up. The swivelling rotor head with adjustable rotor blades makes it possible for a helicopeter to hover or move forwards or backwards. A swivelling, vertically positioned rotor on its tail is used to steer and stabilise the helicopter. Without this stabilising rotor the helicopter would rotate horizontally around the main rotor axle. Changing the angle of the rotor blades and rotor head can also regulate speed. A helicopter can start and land vertically and is used to transport people, in emergencies, for example.

3

Honeycomb construction in rotor blade

2

Control rod
Swash plate
Rotor blade
Rotor gear

Helicopters

Unlike other planes, helicopters can take off and land vertically, fly forwards or backwards and hover in the air.

Even Leonardo da Vinci made early sketches suggesting how an aircraft might climb vertically in the air using a propeller. In 1907 the Frenchman Cornu was the first to have some success with a 'flying bicycle' with which he managed to ascend two metres in the air. He used two paddle-shaped wings to create two-winged rotors. Further experiments were made during the First World War, but those helicopters had to be held in place with ropes. The first 'true' helicopter was built in 1925, and initially included an additional tail propeller. In 1939, Heinrich Focke publically unveiled the first truly navigable helicopter that could stay aloft for more than an hour – the FW 16. It was able to reach a height of over 3,000 metres and speeds of 140 km per hour.

A helicopter has many advantages: it needs no runway for take-off and landing, it can ascend and descend from a standing position and even fly backwards. In order to take off, the rotating wings or 'rotor blades' are set in motion by a turbine engine. The rotating blades create air currents that lift the helicopter vertically. The amount of lift depends on the shape and angle of the rotor blades and their speed of rotation. The speed at which the helicopter takes off can be adjusted by changing the angle at which the blades are set. An additional propeller at the tail of the helicopter or two counter-rotating rotors are used to prevent the helicopter turning against its rotor motion in flight. This makes it possible to keep a steady course. The helicopter can be turned in a particular direction by changing the angle of the rotors. Power is increased when the rotors are not perpendicular to the ground, and the helicopter doesn't only rise but also simultaneously moves forward. Setting the rotors at an angle increases propulsion power.

Regular changes to the angle of the rotor blades above the tail are made with a swash-plate mechanism and control rods. To prevent a helicopter from being overturned by the different forces lifting it up, some models have an inbuilt joint between the rotor blades and rotor head. The rotor blades then oscillate up and down in the course of one revolution. This transfers the torque but prevents the helicopter from overturning. More recent models use elastic rotor blades that are rigidly connected to the rotor head.

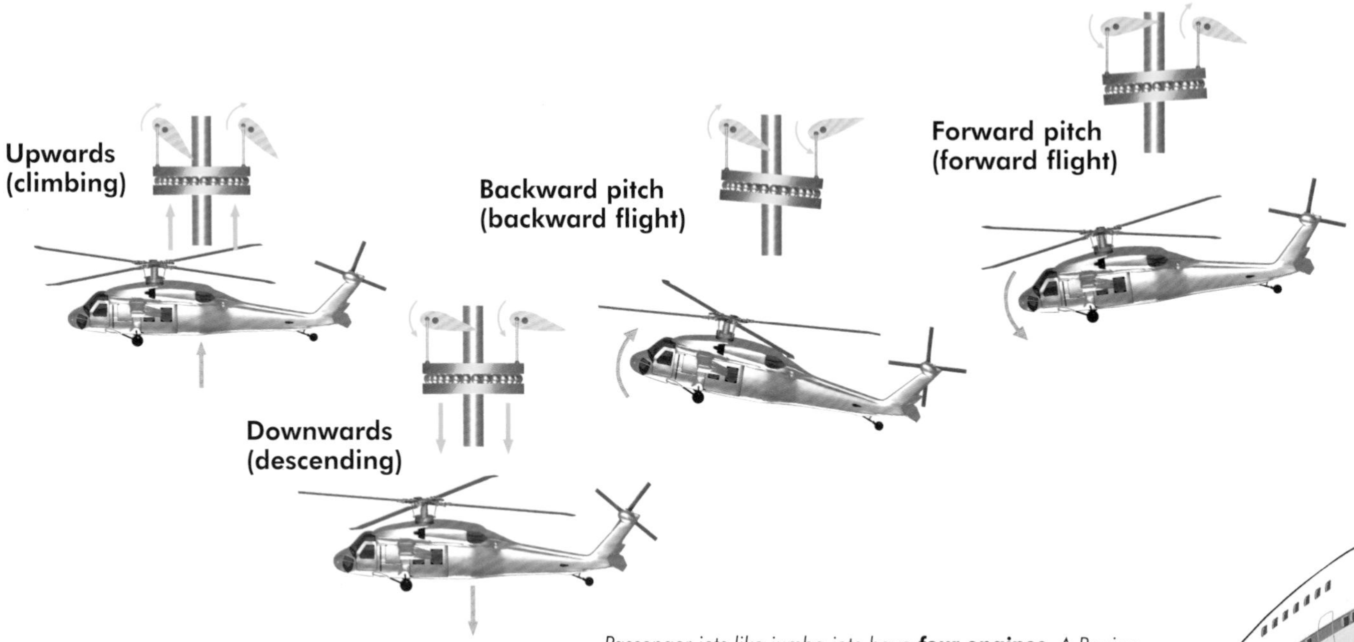

Upwards (climbing)

Backward pitch (backward flight)

Forward pitch (forward flight)

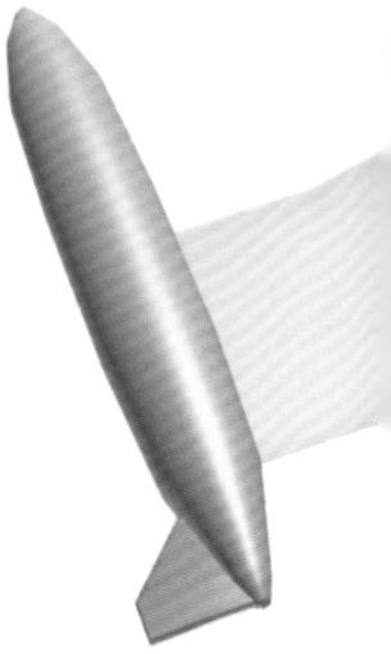

Downwards (descending)

Passenger jets like jumbo jets have **four engines**. A Boeing 747 travelling from London to Hong Kong uses more than 180,000 litres of kerosene for this stretch alone.

Jet planes

Jet planes are powered by jet engines, which convert pressure energy into speed. Jet engines have existed since the end of the Second World War. At that time, they only flew short stretches because of the amount of fuel they needed. The large number of fatal crashes also explains why planes with piston engines were preferred.

Following improvements to the jet engine, the first passenger line service was opened between Johannesburg and London in 1952. The era of the jet engine had begun. Jet engines have become faster and more economical and it is hard to imagine air traffic without them. A mixture of air and fuel is burnt in a jet engine, just like in a car engine, but there are different types of jet engine.

A turbojet has a gas turbine and compressor with giant blades similar to a fan, which suck in air at a common level. Highly pre-compressed air then mixes with a fuel spray of kerosene and paraffin in a combustion chamber and ignites. The burning fuel then heats to a temperature of 1400 °C, keeps expanding, and then blasts out at greater speed through the jet nozzle at the rear of the engine. This thrusts the jet plane and engine forward in the opposite direction to

Aluminium or titanium alloys and steel and nickel compounds are used to build aircraft.

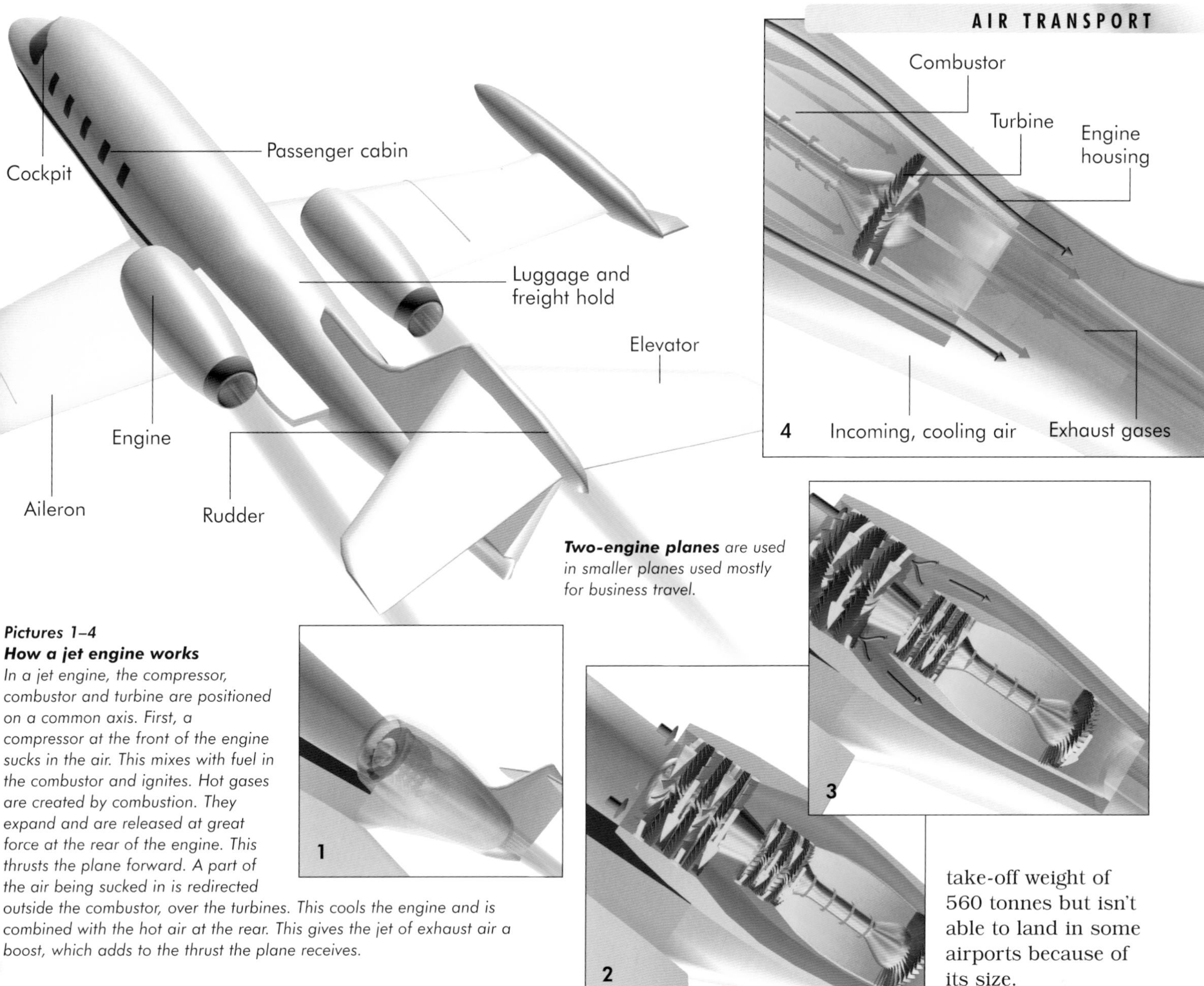

***Two-engine planes** are used in smaller planes used mostly for business travel.*

Pictures 1–4
How a jet engine works
In a jet engine, the compressor, combustor and turbine are positioned on a common axis. First, a compressor at the front of the engine sucks in the air. This mixes with fuel in the combustor and ignites. Hot gases are created by combustion. They expand and are released at great force at the rear of the engine. This thrusts the plane forward. A part of the air being sucked in is redirected outside the combustor, over the turbines. This cools the engine and is combined with the hot air at the rear. This gives the jet of exhaust air a boost, which adds to the thrust the plane receives.

the blast of hot air; the force from the inner walls of the gas turbine is also transferred to the wings and rear of the plane, propelling it forward. Shortly before the hot air is expelled, some of its energy is used to drive a turbine, which regulates the speed at which the air is pressurised by the compressor.

In a turbofan some of the fresh air outside the combustor is redirected before it is mixed with the hot gases to produce greater thrust. Turboprops have an additional propeller driven by a gas turbine. They are suitable for lower speeds and are commonly used for short flights. Ramjets, by contrast, only function at extremely high speeds. The high speeds increase air compression and hence no turbines or compressors are needed. Jet engines make it possible to reach speeds that break the sound barrier. The only passenger plane to break the sound barrier was the Concorde. The Concorde used to fly very high at a speed of over 2,300 km per hour, that is, 2.2 times the speed of sound. The Concorde stopped being built in 1979 and was taken out of service in 2003 after a crash in Paris in 2000.

The biggest civilian passenger jet plane is the double-decker, four-engine Airbus A380 with seats for 853 passengers. It has a maximum take-off weight of 560 tonnes but isn't able to land in some airports because of its size.

Aluminium or titanium alloys and steel and nickel compounds are used to build aircraft.

Space travel

Spaceplanes are manned vehicles that fly into outer space with their payloads. Spaceplanes are reusable, unlike carrier rockets.

In 1981, the successful launch of the *Columbia* marked the beginning of the spaceplane developed by NASA known as the Space Shuttle. Subsequent American missions with the *Challenger*, *Discovery* and *Atlantis* were also successful. Space Shuttle flights ended abruptly when the *Challenger* broke up 73 seconds after its launch and all seven crewmembers died. It was two years before flights resumed, with the *Discovery*. In 2003, NASA also lost the *Columbia*. A defective heat shield resulted in it breaking up at a height of 60 km and once again all seven crewmembers were lost. The last Space Shuttle flight was launched in 2011 but there are plans for new American spaceships. The 'Buran', launched into orbit by a carrier rocket, was the first spaceship to be developed by the former Soviet Union.

The Space Shuttle had three main components: orbiter, external tank and solid rocket booster. The orbiter was the most important component. Following a mission, the orbiter would land on Earth, descending at a speed of about 370 km per hour, similar to an airplane. A thermal protection system made of a combination of ceramic, glass and carbon shielded it from the extreme heat (up to 1,600 °C) experienced on re-entry into the Earth's atmosphere. Several engines were used for its propulsion and navigation. It had space for seven astronauts.

Orbiter

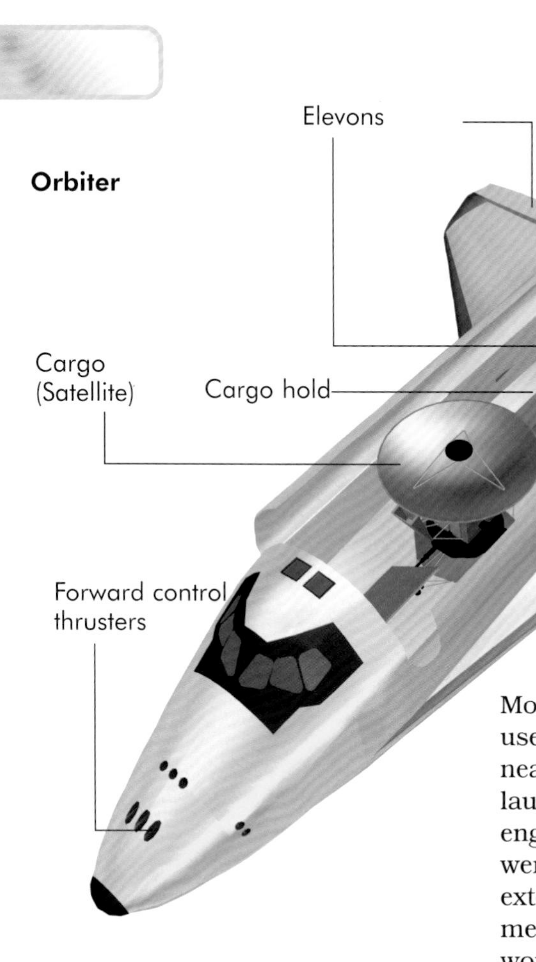

Spaceplane launch

Most of the space was used for a cargo of nearly 30,000 kg. To launch it, the main engines of the orbiters were fuelled by the external tank some 50 metres high. The tank would detach itself and burn up on entering the atmosphere. Two enormous solid rocket boosters on its flanks provided the additional boost needed to launch the 2,000-tonne Shuttle. The boosters would detach themselves when they were empty and fall to Earth with parachutes so they could be reused.

Manned and unmanned Space Shuttles and spaceplanes are mainly used for scientific research. They also transport news, weather and navigation satellites into outer space.

Rockets

Rockets are craft propelled by thrust. The first rockets were used in battle in China as early as the 12th century. Gunpowder was used to obtain the power needed to fire them. Rockets were also used in the 19th century during the Anglo-American war; however, they could only travel a distance of 2 km. The first real breakthrough came with the invention of liquid-propellant rockets by the physicist Goddard in 1926.

Rockets are propelled by thrust, a force described by Isaac Newton in his Law of Action and Reaction: for every action, there is an equal and opposite reaction. If expanding gases are pushed through a nozzle with great force, the opposing forces will create a thrust to propel a rocket.

Flares and fireworks are examples of the simplest kind of rocket. Larger rockets are composed of a rocket engine, navigation systems, control mechanisms and body-tube, with a payload section to transport crew, research equipment, explosive charges or space probes. There isn't enough oxygen at high altitudes to burn fuel for rockets, so liquid propellants such as hydrogen or kerosene and an oxidiser, carried in separate tanks, are used instead. The amount of thrust depends on the quantity and speed at which the fuel is released. Multi-stage rockets can reach particularly high altitudes. Each unit or stage has a fuel tank and engine with a thrust chamber and fuel injection system. When the fuel in one unit gets used up, it detaches itself and the next engine starts up.

Solid fuel is also used in some rocket systems. Compared to liquid-fuel rockets, solid-fuel combustion chambers have a relatively small energy content and a shorter life. Solid-fuel rockets are used for military purposes or as boosters.

19th century caricature of a steam-powered rocket

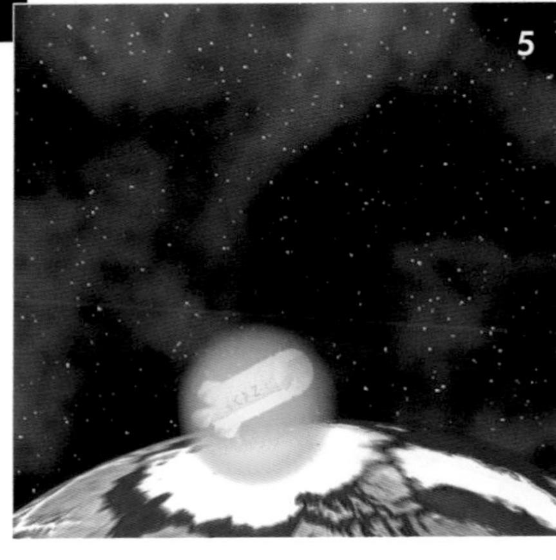

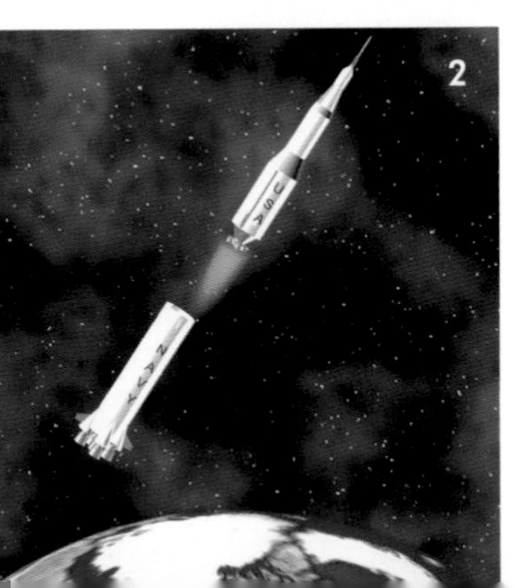

Pictures 1–5

A space rocket is launched into outer space from a ramp. The conquest of outer space began on 4 October 1957 when the Soviet Sputnik rocket was launched. A rocket engine consists of a combustion chamber with either solid or liquid fuel and a nozzle. When the fuel is burned gases are squeezed out through the nozzle, giving the rocket thrust. Space rockets have several tiers or stages. The rockets are steered by smaller rockets, which burn for short periods of time.

CHAPTER 5

Ships

Boats and ships transport people and goods on rivers, lakes and seas. The size and shape of boats and ships, and how they are equipped, can be very different, depending on their use.

Early ships and boats relied on the wind and on muscle power. As technology progressed, steam, diesel and even nuclear power have been used to power ships. The first boats were made of tree trunks and rafts propelled by using paddles. Sailing ships made it possible to cover long distances by making use of the power of wind. The use of sailing ships declined with the introduction of the paddle steamer at the start of the 19th century. Then, wooden hulls began to be replaced by iron ones and propellers increasingly replaced paddles. The first ocean liners with steam engines appeared in the mid-19th century.

Nowadays, most ships are powered by steam turbines or diesel engines. Large ships include containers, freighters and tankers, as well as passenger ships. Hydrofoils and hovercraft are built so that they can be lifted out of the water and travel at high speeds. Submarines are used for military and research purposes; the earliest models were in use as early as the end of the 18th century.

Sailing ships

Sailing ships are driven by wind to move across water. Before the steam engine, apart from using muscle power, this was the only way to move across water.

The Egyptians used rowing ships with square sails on the Nile as early as 6000 BC. From 3000 BC sailing boats crossed the Mediterranean for trade. In 800 BC the Phoenicians used round ships for goods and narrow longships in battle. Over the next centuries triangular sails, jibs and topsails began to be used. In the 19th century sailing ships with masts for up to seven overlapping sails were built. The fastest sailing ships were clippers. They were used to ship tea from the 1850s, and from 1915 also took passengers around Cape Horn. The biggest wooden ship was the *Great Republic*. It was 99 metres long and was launched in 1853. Sailing ships fell out of use with the invention of the steam engine. Today, sailing boats and a few sailing ships are only used for sport. They are usually made of light synthetic materials and aluminium. Sails, originally made of cotton or hemp, are now made of more waterproof and tougher synthetic fibres.

In a triangular mainsail the edges are known as the luff, foot and leech. Round, wooden poles known as 'battens' are used in 'batten pockets' to strengthen the sails. 'Reef points' are used to reduce the area of a sail. Square sails, on the other hand, are rectangular sails attached to round wooden 'spars' or 'yard-arms' and hung horizontally from the mast. Ships with such sails are known as 'square-riggers'. The tall ship *Gorch Fock* is an example of a square-rigger.

In a 'fore-and-aft sail' the sail is set parallel to the ship's keel. Gaff sails, bermuda sails, lateen sails and spritsails are all different types of 'fore-and-aft sails'. There are also many kinds of light sail and they are used as additional sails in particular wind conditions.

The position and size of a sail can be adjusted to keep a sailing boat on course by manipulating the lines in the rigging.

Sailboat

English sailing ship from 1588

Sport motorboat

Motor ships

Cruise ships
Few ocean liners exist today; they became less important with the advent of airlines. Nonetheless, many large ships are still being built and they are all cruise ships. More than 300 are in use today worldwide.

A motor ship is a ship driven by a combustion engine, which is usually a diesel engine.

Modern shipping took off in the 19th century with the use of steam-powered ships built of iron and steel. Steam paddles like the *Clermont* built by Robert Fulton were the first steam-powered vessels. In 1807 Fulton undertook the first 'big' journey with passengers between New York and

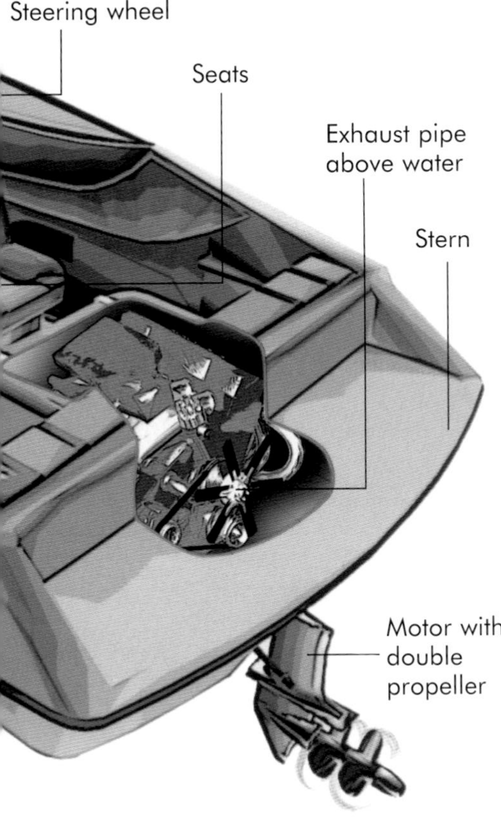

Albany on the Hudson River. Paddle steamers worked well on rivers but weren't that well suited to sea travel. The first iron steam-ships were introduced in 1820 followed by motor ships with diesel engines in 1903.

Motor ships with diesel engines have proven their worth. A diesel engine is economic to run and doesn't need boiler systems. Diesel engines continue to be used even in newer ships. A diesel engine rotates slowly enough to directly power the ship's propeller and no separate gears are needed. A ship's propeller is usually positioned at the stern, below the water line, and connected to the engine by a propeller shaft, which rotates it. The propeller blades push the water backwards and the ship is propelled forward by the resulting counterforce.

The speed of the ship depends on the propeller's revolutions per minute and the shape of its blades. Like aeroplane wings, the propeller blades are bowed in order to transmit power better. The blade angles can be adjusted in some propellers, making it possible to reverse. Some propeller designs even make it possible to move a ship sideways.

Ships are assembled in shipyards in so-called 'shipways' using prefabricated hull parts that are welded together, and the engine is built in. Boats made from light materials can float on the water independently, but large ships need empty air-filled compartments to keep them on the water surface. To prevent the ship sinking in case of a leak, watertight doors separate compartments in the hull so that water from a leak is restricted to a small area of the ship and the ship can stay afloat. A ship's cargo has to be distributed evenly and secured so that the ship doesn't capsize in stormy weather.

Today, more and more cruise ships of increasing size are being built. They even have theatres and shopping malls. A mega-ship can carry over 2,000 passengers. The biggest cruise ship currently is *The Allure of the Seas* with capacity for 6,300 passengers.

Ferry

Hydrofoils *have a wing-like structure below the hull. The dynamic uplift created by this shape lifts the body of the boat out of the water at accelerating speeds, thereby reducing friction.*

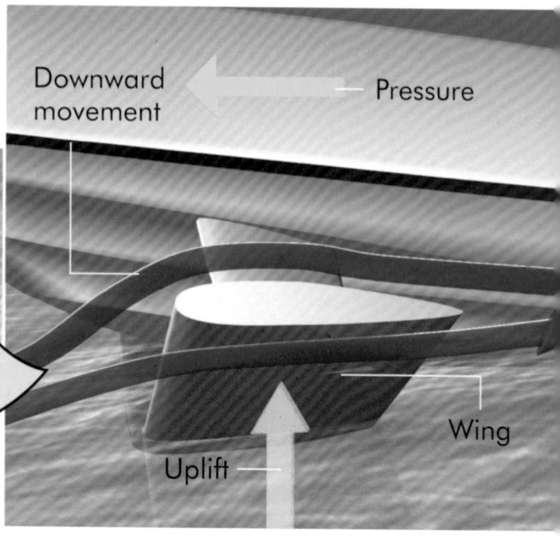

Hydrofoils

Hydrofoils are boats with wings attached to the hull. The body of the boat is lifted out of the water at high speeds using aerodynamic principles similar to those of an aeroplane.

In conventional ships, were the hull sits below the water, the amount of water displaced and the friction created with water during acceleration limit the speed they can reach to 25 knots (45 km per hour). 1 knot is equivalent to 1.85 km.

Hydrofoils, by contrast can reach speeds of 80 knots and more, and are usually used to carry passengers on rivers or in coastal areas.Rigid or hinged wings are attached to the hydrofoil below the hull, diagonal to the direction of travel. The part of the hull that is submerged in the water is similar to the hull of other motorboats. When docked or moving at slow speed, a hydrofoil floats on the water like any other boat. On acceleration, at higher speeds the wings create uplift and the hull is lifted higher and higher out of the water until the wings simply glide through the water. Such high speeds are possible because there is much less friction.

Hyrdofoils use propellers or thrust for propulsion. In the latter case, water is sucked in at the bow of the boat and then expelled with great force through a nozzle at the stern. Hydrofoils are not built for use on the high seas, where the sudden submersion of the wings in water could result in serious damage to the boat's structure or even tear it apart.

Hydrofoil (conventional propeller propulsion)

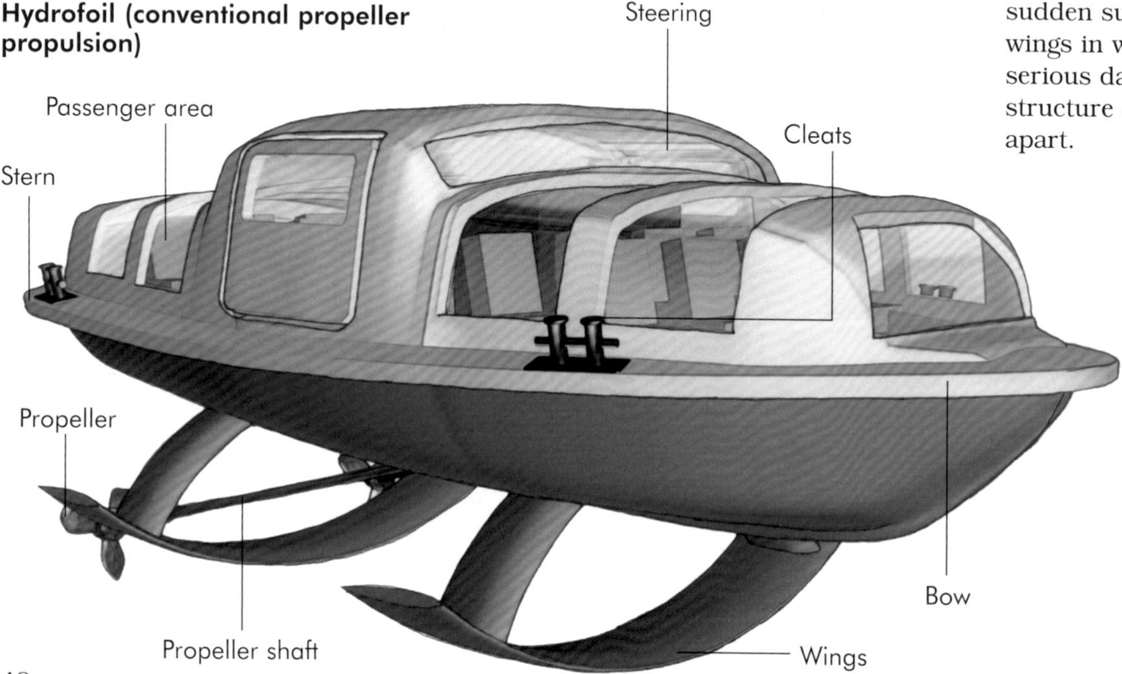

Cargo ships

Aircraft carriers were built to make it easier for aeroplanes to reach the area of operation in wartime. They made it possible to take off and land at sea.

Cargo ships transport goods. Their shape and equipment depend on their purpose.

Cargo ships come in different sizes depending on the kind of goods being transported. They usual have large diesel engines with a low rate of revolutions per minute. To cool the enormous engines, water is taken up on one side of the ship, piped through the engine block, and then let out on the other side of the ship. The steam created in this cooling process is simultaneously used to ensure a supply of hot water. A rudder connected to the ship's propeller is used to steer the ship. It determines the direction of the stream created by the rudder. In shallow waters the ship is steered by a 'bowthruster'.

Container ships that travel on seas all over the world transport goods in standardised metal containers made for transporting large volumes of goods. Lorries or trains to specific container terminals in ports deliver the containers and they are then loaded onto the ships by cranes, which are sometimes part of the ships.

Container ships have large loading decks with guide rails to secure the loads. The cargo is stacked in the containers in multiple layers.

Similar to containers are 'lighter aboard' or LASH ships. These ships take aboard loading barges or 'lighters' on a specially designed stern. General cargo vessels transport individually packaged goods. These can include a wide range of goods that are stored in separate cargo holds. Bulk carriers transport ore, cement, grain and other loose products in cargo holds with their own hatches. The cargo is dropped loose, and without any packaging, directly into the hold on conveyor belts or through tubes.

Oil is transported in enormous, specially designed tankers. Almost the entire hull, divided by watertight doors, is filled with oil. The partitions prevent the tanker from becoming unbalanced as the oil sloshes about. Oil tankers can be as large as 450 metres in length and 50 metres wide. They have the capacity to carry huge quantities of crude oil and are only permitted in specific ports with special facilities. Some oil tankers have been the cause of devastating environmental disasters where vast areas of coastland have been contaminated by oil spillages. Specialised tankers are also used for the transport of natural gas, wines or liquid chemicals.

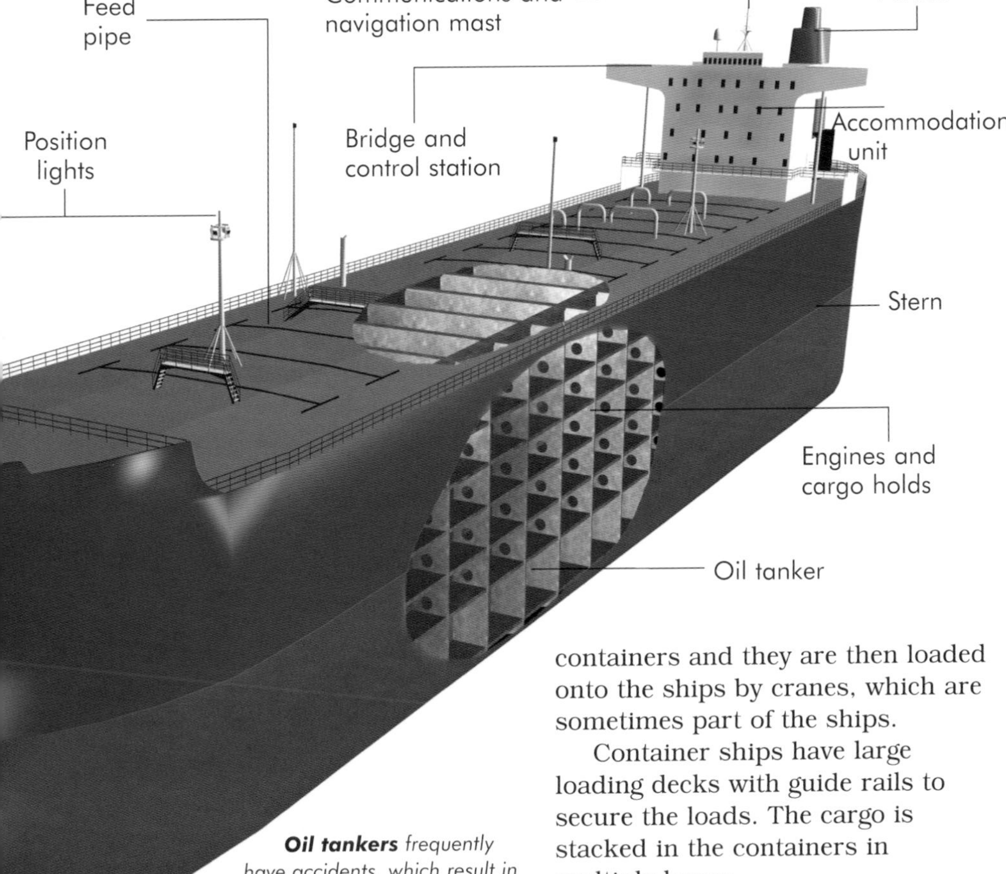

***Oil tankers** frequently have accidents, which result in marine and coastal oil pollution.*

Hovercraft

Hovercraft float or hover with the help of an air cushion between the craft and the land or sea.

A patent for an air cushion as a means to reduce friction between a ship's hull and water was granted as far back as 1877. In 1955 C. Cockrell acquired a patent for the first hovercraft. After the establishment of Hovercraft Development Ltd, initial trials with hovercraft were made in the English Channel in 1959 and they finally developed into a hovercraft service operating between Dover and Calais. The craft were nearly 50 metres long and 20 metres wide, with capacity for 400 passengers and approximately 80 passenger cars. They could reach speeds of 130 km per hour depending on wind conditions and wave height.

In order to lift up the craft, air is pumped into a rubber skirt around the craft using special air compressors. The skirt sits under the boat and on the surface. To prevent air escaping with the motion of every wave, a row of 'fingers' around the skirt creates a seal.

Hovercrafts use powerful engines that are not too heavy for propulsion. They require considerable thrust to propel the weight of the craft. Smaller craft use robust diesel engines. Larger craft use jet engines. Dynamic fans on the bow and stern enable forward propulsion and steering. They also make use of air released through tiny openings in the sidewalls in order to steer.

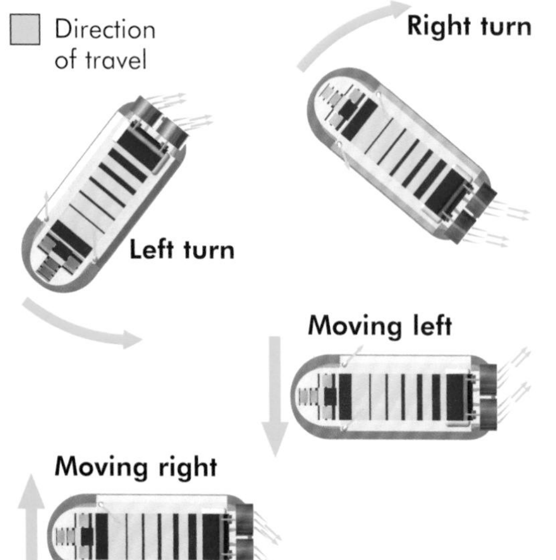

*A **hovercraft** can glide over firm ground and water on an air cushion. The flexibility of the air cushion makes smooth journeys possible even in rough seas and over uneven surfaces. The requisite air pressure is produced with the aid of high-performance fans. The skirt prevents air leaking from the air cushion. The fans are driven by thrust and the boat can be steered by adjusting the position of the fans.*

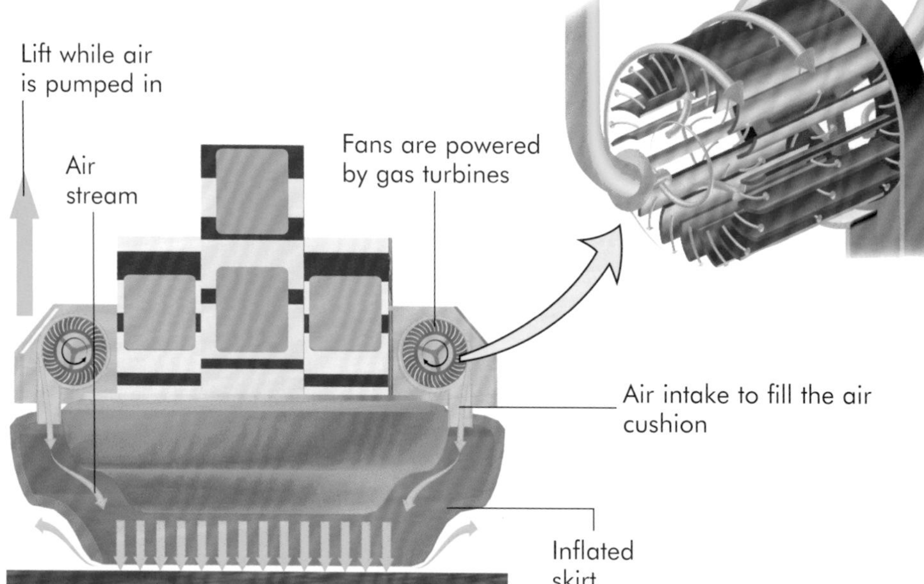

Submarines

Submarines are almost exclusively used for underwater military purposes. They have the advantage of being hard to find once submerged.

Early submarines were invented as early as the beginning of the 17th century and made of wooden rowing boats encased in leather. Drebbel, a Dutchman, is credited with inventing such a boat, which, rowed by 12 men, remained submerged in the Thames for a few hours. Pipes reaching above the surface of the water provided oxygen. A modern version built in 1800 by Robert Fulton was the *Nautilus*. Oxygen was supplied underwater from compressed air and it had rudders for depth and lateral control. A hand-operated screw propeller with four vanes was used for propulsion, and sails were used when above water.

Modern submarines consist of pressure-proof hulls with a circular cross-section, enabling them to withstand high pressure. The inner hull is reinforced with struts or 'ribs'. In order to dive, water is pumped into ballast tanks inside the hull until the submarine reaches the desired depth. To resurface, water is pumped out of the tanks by using compressed air. Hydroplanes on the bow and stern help the submarine to resurface and to maintain depth.

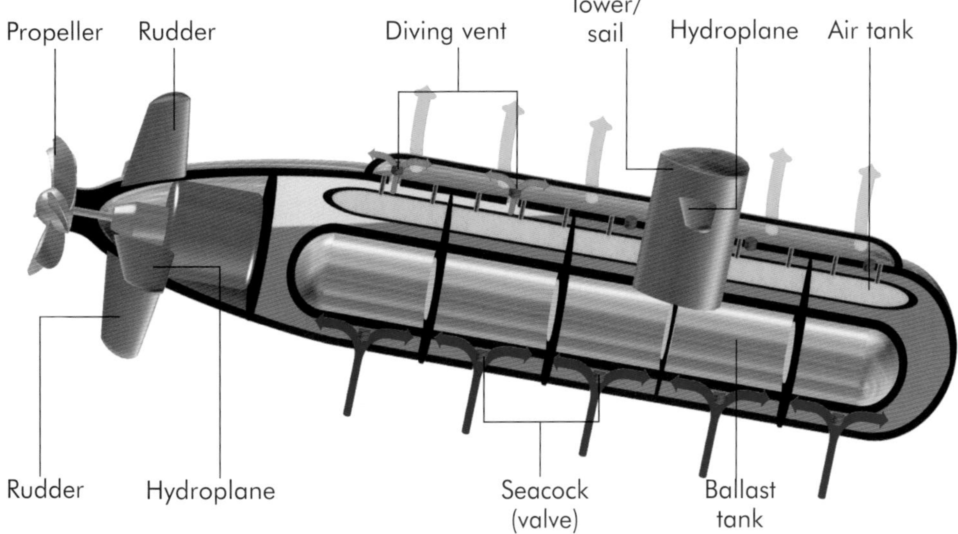

A tower on the hull, also known as the 'sail' or 'fin', houses the entrance hatch, periscope and communications mast, although the latter cannot be used under water since electromagnetic waves cannot be received underwater. Radar and ultrasound are used for navigation.

Submarines are powered by diesel engines and electric power from batteries. Nuclear reactors driving turbines are also used, making it possible to travel long distances. An accident in a nuclear submarine would release an enormous amount of radioactivity into the ocean, however.

German submarine cruiser

Submarine ballast tank

Ballast tanks are located in the inner hull of a submarine, which has a double wall. They are hollow chambers in the wall of the submarine that can be pumped full of air or water via a valve. When a submarine needs to surface the walls are filled with compressed air, and with water when it needs to dive. Hydroplanes support the submarine when submerged. The amount of water or air needed in the ballast tanks depends on the depth of the submarine. When the tanks are completely full of air the sub will float on the surface. Propellers are used for propulsion.

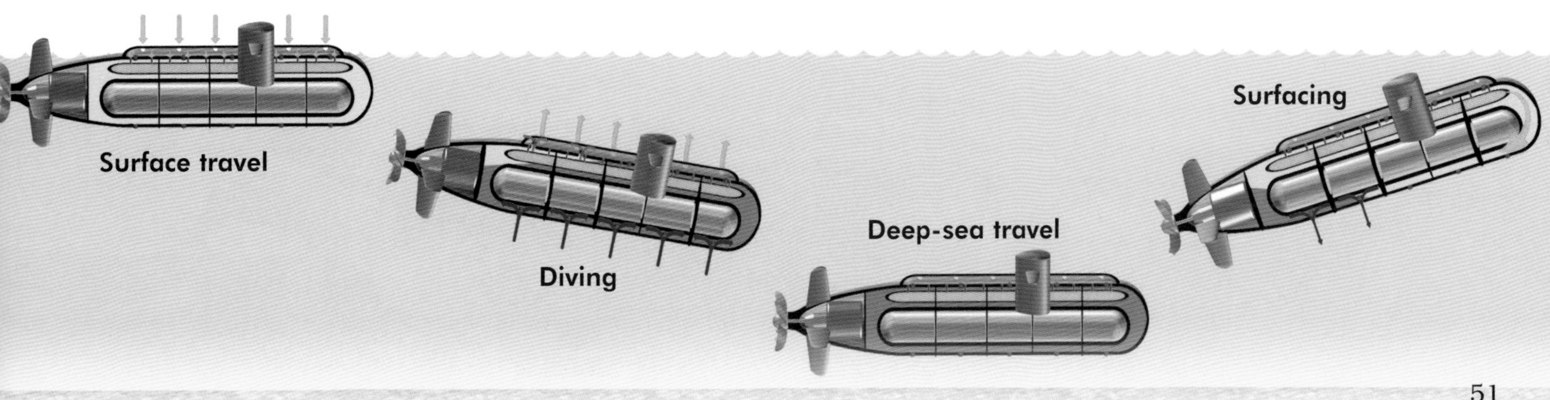

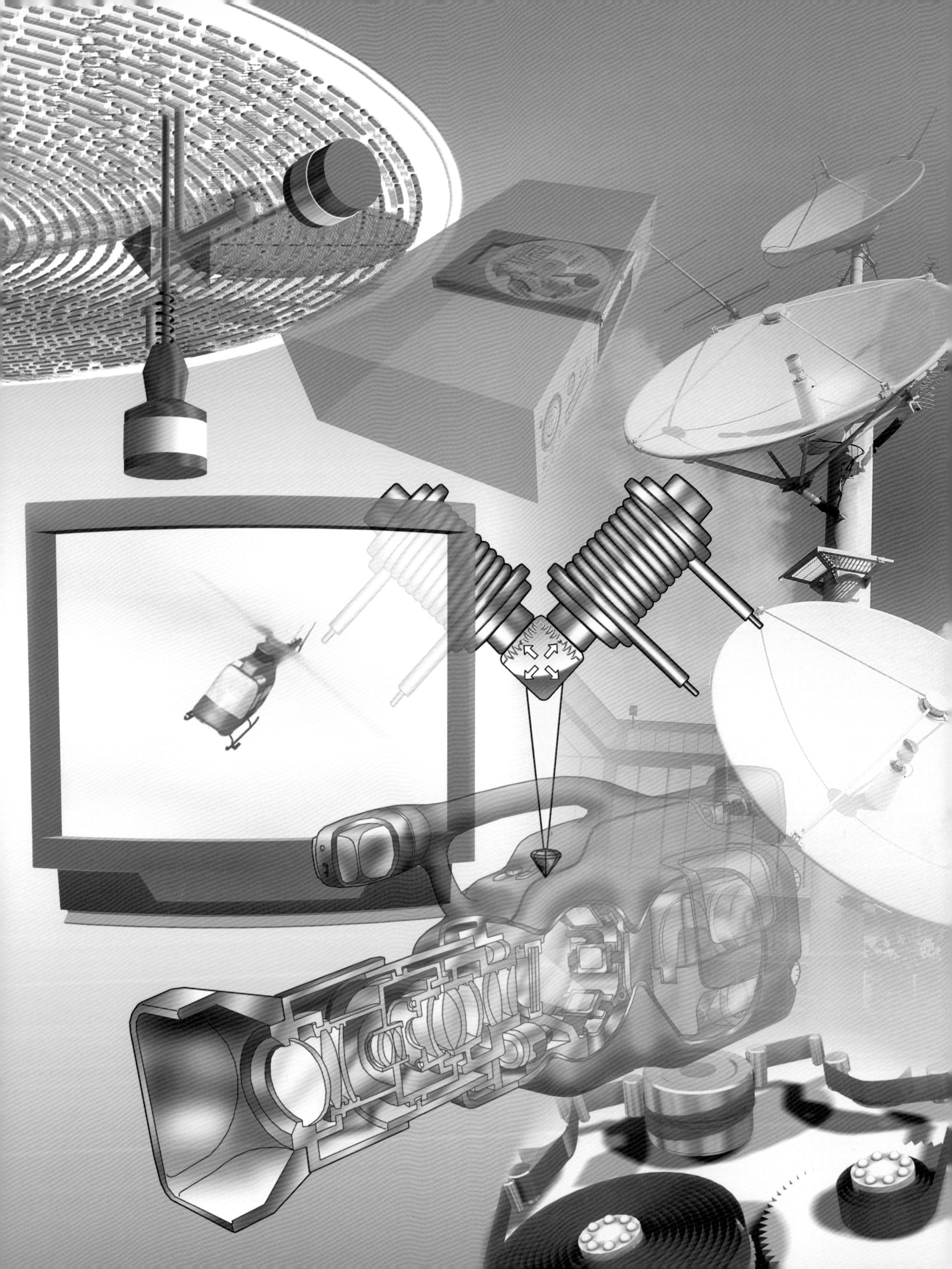

CHAPTER 6

Audio and video systems

About a hundred years ago, if you wanted to hear music you had to go to a concert; if you wanted to hear recent news you had to go a gathering of some kind.

The path leading to today's audio and video systems runs through the entire history of humankind. At first human beings used only their speech for communication, then they began to draw and paint on walls. The development of writing came next, followed by the invention of printing, which made it possible to duplicate an almost infinite number of copies of an original piece of information. In addition, documents and books can and could be transported far and wide.

Until the 1950s vacuum 'valves' were used for radios. These were followed by smaller and cheaper transistor radios. Sound has been recorded on vinyl records, cassettes and CDs, and in digital formats such as MP3 in different digital recording media.

The most common audio-visual devices and systems used today are the television and the Internet. The first British television broadcast was made by Baird in 1929. Before television, moving pictures were available as films and there was the theatre. Silent movies were shown from 1895 onwards, and were replaced with the introduction of sound in 1927. Video technology made home movies possible. Digitalisation of moving pictures has made it possible to watch almost any film or programme at home in high quality, whether on DVD/Blu-ray or via the Internet, where numerous videos can be seen, or from which films can be downloaded onto personal computers.

Radio

Radios are used to transmit and receive electromagnetic waves to generate acoustic signals.

Rudolf Hertz is seen as the founder of radio technology. In 1888 he demonstrated the existence of electromagnetic waves. In 1902 the Italian G. Marconi (1874–1937) succeeded in sending wireless signals across the Atlantic. A few years later the broadcast of the Christmas story with accompanying background gramophone music (received over a distance of 300 km) was considered a spectacular event.

After the First World War, the invention of the transistor, used as an amplifier, was a big step forward leading to radio broadcasting and the radio. Many kinds of radio are available today: radio alarm clocks, car radios, music systems with built-in radios, or mobile phones with radios. Analog radios use a high-frequency generator such as an oscillator circuit to create the frequencies necessary for transmission. An oscillator circuit consists of a capacitor and a coil, which can store energy. The energy in the oscillating current travels back and forth between capacitor and coil. The electrons oscillate at a given frequency depending on the size of the coil and the capacitor.

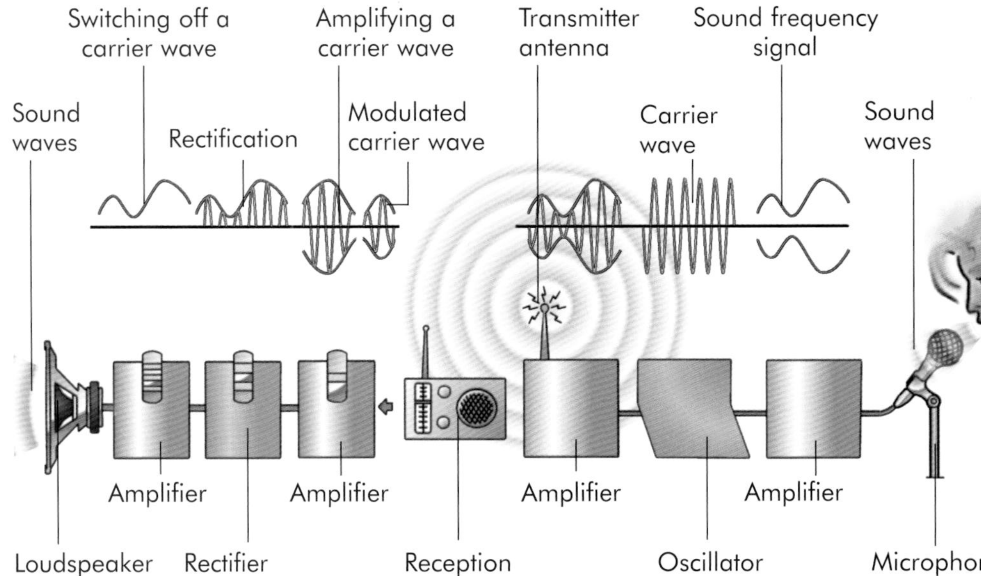

Sound waves

When a radio programme is transmitted, sound is converted into electric voltage, which changes according to the original sound produced. The length of a carrier wave can be shortened by an amount corresponding to the voltage. The exactly opposite process takes place in the receiver so that sounds and speech can be played out of a loudspeaker at home. An exact reconversion is only possible because the carrier frequency has a defined and fixed length that is recognisably the same for the transmitter and the receiver.

A transmitting antenna and a receiving antenna each make up an oscillatory circuit. If a circuit generator (an oscillator) is connected to an antenna at the same frequency, the antenna receives energy. The waves produced in the electromagnetic field created by this process travel at the speed of light. The sound waves of music and speech are first converted into fluctuating frequencies via a microphone and then transmitted to a receiver by a carrier wave. When they are being received, carrier waves from other senders have to be blocked, so a particular carrier frequency has to be selected on a radio. Once selected, the electrically relayed message has to be demodulated (extracted from the carrier wave) and then retransmitted as sound waves in a loudspeaker on the receiver. Buildings or mountains can interfere with reception, resulting in hissing and crackling. This doesn't happen with a digital radio, however, since the signals are sent to the receiver as digital codes in small data packets; in fact, each packet is sent several times to ensure clear reception.

Radio waves are used to transmit sound signals. In the field of radio broadcasting, short, long, medium and ultra short waves are used. Their ranges are as different as their characteristics.

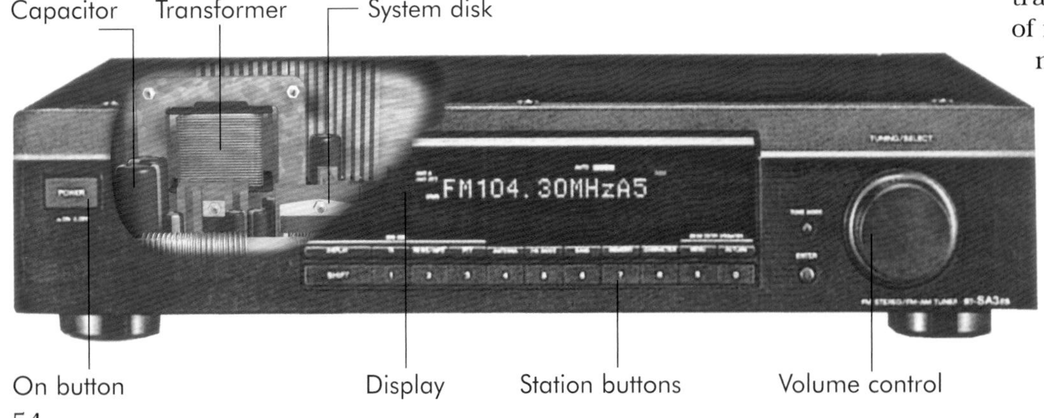

Television

Television involves the transmission of moving images. This is possible when the images are broken down into individual points that are then converted into electrical impulses.

As far back as 1843 people knew that an image field had to be broken up in order to transmit it electrically. In 1884 the German Paul Gottlieb Nipkow acquired a patent for his Nipkow disc. It was a disc with a series of holes. By placing the disc in front of your eye and rotating it, you would see a line starting from one of the holes at the top, followed by other lines forming below, until the entire image had been scanned. Later, in 1906, a cathode ray tube known as 'Braun's tube' was developed by Max Dieckmann. In 1930 M. von Ardenne presented the first completely electronic television picture. In 1952 Nord-West-Deutscher Rundfunk (the North-West German Radio Broadcasting service) began offering public-service television. The official colour encoding system used for colour televison since 1967 and still in use is the PAL (short for Phase Alternating Line) system developed by Telefunken.

An LCD (liquid-crystal display) screen builds up an image from small dots called pixels. A single pixel is made up of three sub-pixels in the basic colours of blue, red and green. In the background a constantly lit white light sends out rays through tiny liquid crystals. Each sub-pixel has its own transistor – a switching element. An electric current ensures that the individual crystals realign themselves and the sub-pixels switch on or off and transmit light differently. The human eye reassembles the pixels into a complete image.

For a long time television sets were exclusively cathode ray tube televisions. In these televisions, an electron beam was produced in the cathode ray tube at the back of the television. The cathode ray hit the screen from behind and lit it up at that particular point. Other points on the screen remained dark – you could think of it like a sieve. Deflection coils then directed the ray, line by line, onto the screen so that the human eye would perceive all the illuminated dots as a composite image.

Cathode ray televisions and computer monitors have since been replaced almost completely by flat LCD or plasma screens. These take up less space and require less energy and can also receive digital and high-definition television programmes (HDTV). Programmes today are frequently digitised and transmitted as data packets whose data size is reduced using MPEG compression. In Europe programmes are received via DVB-T (Digital Video Broadcasting–Terrestrial). They are sometimes locked (Pay-TV) and a decoder is needed to see them. Along with the rise of HD and 3D television sets, television broadcasting is increasingly being networked via the Internet.

LCD screens and plasma screens are two different kinds of flat screen. In plasma screens, gas is 'ignited' in numerous small chambers so the fluorescence makes the colours visible.

DVDs and Blu-ray Discs

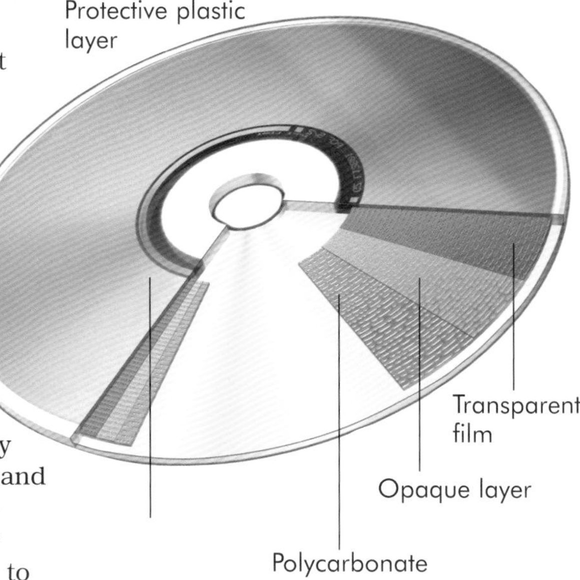

A DVD looks similar to a CD but has a much bigger memory (between 4.7 and 17 GB). DVDs were originally developed to save and store films (DVD = Digital Video Disc) but since they were also being used to store other kinds of data, DVD now stands for Digital Versatile Disc. As a storage medium for films, the DVD and DVD player have completely replaced the video cassette and video recorder. Films can be viewed in much better quality and there is no need to rewind to find a particular spot in a film as scenes can be selected directly. The rise in DVD burners and DVD recorders since the end of the 1990s has also made individual recording of films or other data on DVD possible. Recordable DVDs are used for this purpose (e.g. DVD-R or DVD-RW for rewritable DVDs).

Hard drive recorders, which record data straight onto a hard disk, became established for recording TV programmes, finally sealing the fate of the video recorder. A DVD can be played on either side. It is made of two parts that are glued together back-to-back. Each side has a double-layer recording capacity, which means that each disk has a total of four storage areas. The surface of each layer is covered with a transparent film that a laser can 'see through' to read information from the bottom layer. To ensure the DVD runs smoothly, one layer is written and read in a spiral from inside moving outwards and the other layer starts from the outside.

Blu-ray Discs have even greater storage capacity: 25 to 128 GB. They are mainly used to store high-definition films, which would not fit on a DVD.

The pits and lands in a Blu-ray Disc are even closer together and are read by a blue laser (hence the name of the disks). The laser wavelength is shorter than a DVD laser, as is the distance between laser and disk. All these elements make denser data storage possible.

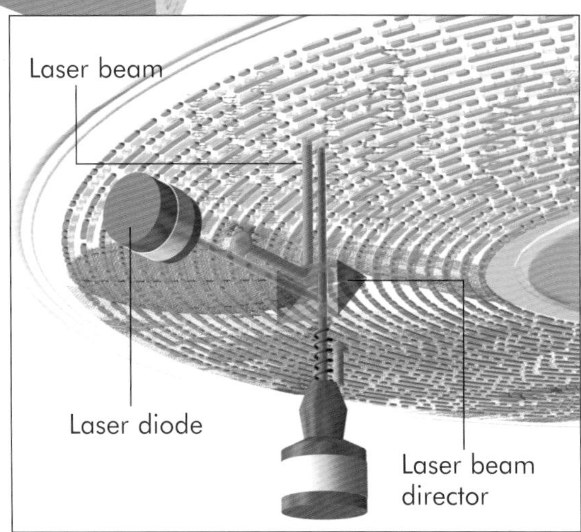

Just like in a CD, a DVD has indentations in its surface ('pits') arranged as spiral tracks. The non-indented surfaces are called 'lands'. Pits and lands are more closely packed in a DVD than in a CD. A laser beam scans them. Lands reflect the light from the beam and the pits absorb or scatter it. The tracks of the pits are made up of sectors with 'headers' containing information on the identification, specification and error detection separately from the music and film data stored. The reflected laser beams are captured and converted into a digital data stream by a detector. The data then appears on the screen via the player's electronic system.

Record players

*In 1888, Emil Berliner developed **the gramophone** – the forerunner of the record player. It was driven by a spring mechanism that was wound up by a crank. A flat disc was initially used as the sound carrier but a funnel was added to improve sound.*

A record player is a device that replays the sounds stored on a record.

Following several unsuccessful attempts to record sound, the American inventor Thomas A. Edison developed the first phonograph in 1877. He did this by using a cylinder coated with tin foil or wax. Sound vibrations were engraved into the coating in a spiral form by a sharp needle attached to a membrane. To replay the sounds a needle retraced the grooves and the sound was replayed through the vibrating membrane. The device was initially intended as a dictation machine. Ten years later, Emil Berliner replaced the cylinder with a disc-shaped record with spiral grooves of different heights and depths. A few years later it was possible to duplicate the discs. Mass production began using shellac instead of hard rubber. The early 'gramophone' was initially driven by using a hand-operated crank, and later a spring mechanism. Electric recording and playback, which significantly improved sound quality, were the next big steps. As shellac was replaced by synthetic material, records with microgrooves were produced to enable longer playing time, resulting in the LPs that are produced today.

A record player consists of an electrically driven motor, a pick-up arm, turntable, needle and amplifier. The turntable is a flat disc on which the record rests, rotating at an even speed and driven by the motor. A needle with a gemstone tip on one end of the pick-up arm is placed in the record groove. Most players have pick-up arms which automatically place and lift the needles. Pick-up arms make it possible to gently place and lift the needle at any position on a record. The different heights and depths of the grooves cause the needle to vibrate. The vibrations are converted into electrical impulses by an electromechanical convertor in the pick-up arm, and are then amplified and replayed through a loudspeaker.

With advances in technology, crystal needle systems are being replaced with magnetic pick-ups. Although record players are no longer common for everyday use, they continue to be popular with DJs. Specialised record players with variable turntable speeds and powerful motors enable techniques such as *scratching* (swivelling a record back and forth while it's playing) or *backspin* (swivelling a record backwards at speed).

Crystal stylus needle

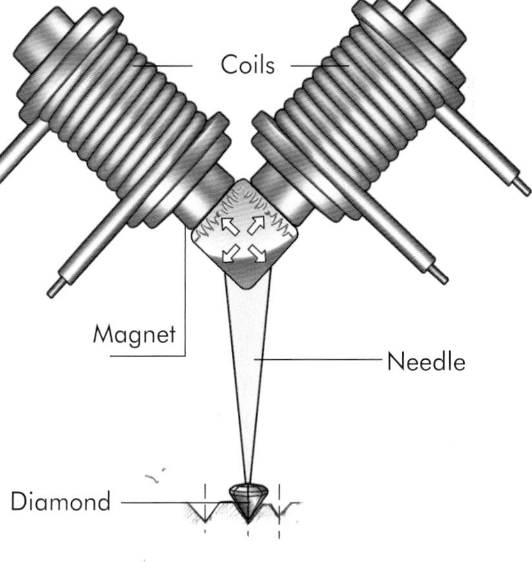

CD players

CD players are playback devices for CDs (Compact Discs), which, like DVD players, use laser beams to read the discs. The stored information is converted into electrical impulses and then into sound waves via a loudspeaker.

For their use in audio systems, the CD is a further development of the record. It is smaller and has greater recording capacity than a conventional record. The biggest advantage of a CD over a record is that it doesn't wear out and it retains its good sound quality. Synthetic metallised discs are used as sound carriers. Sound, or rather the vibrations, are digitally stored as small indentations known as 'pits'. The discs are then coated with an extremely thin film of aluminium and an additional protective coating.

A system of mirrors and lenses generates a sharply focused laser beam that scans and reads the CD. The sharp focus is very important since the soundtracks are only 1.6 thousandths of a millimetre apart. The indentations are each only 0.5 thousandths of millimetre wide and only a few thousandths of a millimetre long. The laser beam's reflection in the indentations and flat areas of the CD varies. The laser beam is only reflected back from a flat area. The reflected beam is then detected by a light sensor (detector) and converted into electrical impulses. A digital–analog converter turns the impulses into electrical vibrations, and they then become audible as sound through a loudspeaker. The speed at which a laser beam reads a disc is around 1.2 meters per second. This is equivalent to about 500 revolutions per minute in the middle of the CD and 200 r.p.m at the edge. With the widespread popularity of CD burners almost every computer user now uses rewriteable blank CDs to store music as well as all kinds of other data.

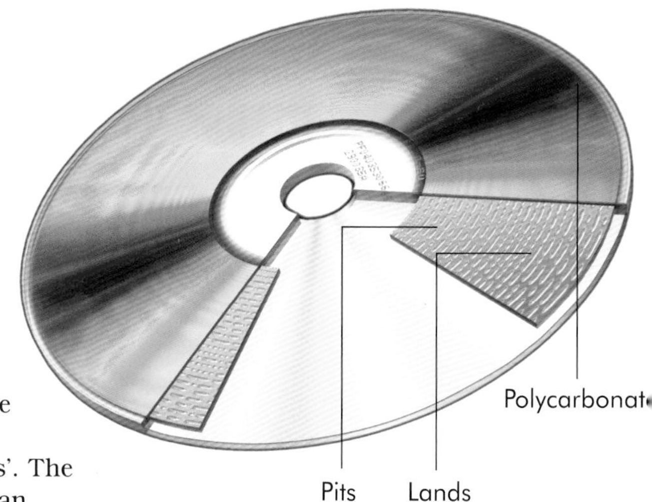

Pits and lands
Just like a DVD a CD also has spirally arranged 'pits' in which sound signals are stored, and 'lands' (the unindented areas).

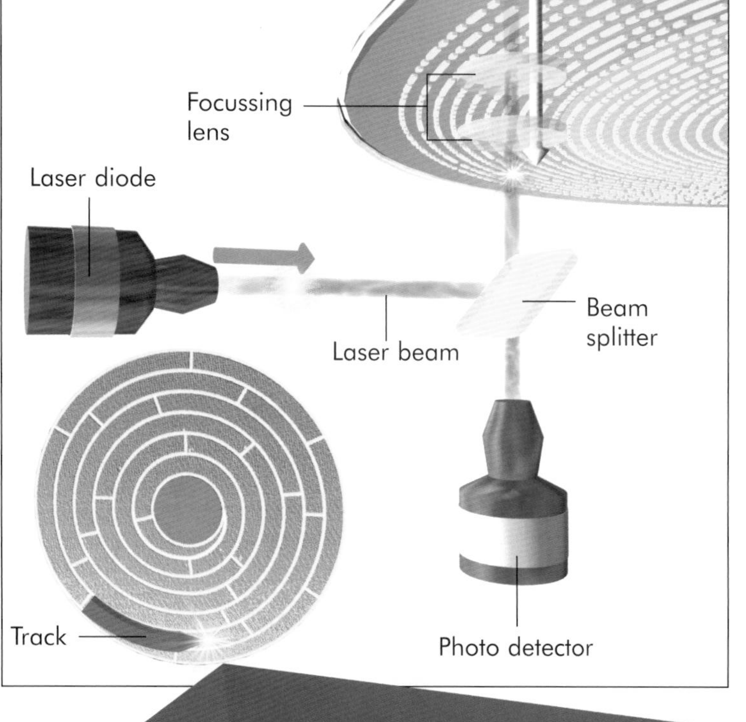

Laser beams in CD players
CD players enable trouble free playback of a compact disc with music without wear and tear. During playback, the CD itself rotates while the laser beam simultaneously moves over all the tracks storing information, from the middle of the disc outwards. This sharply focussed laser beam is directed onto the surface of the CD via a system of mirrors and lenses. It scans the indentations on the CD which hold the information. A light-sensitive detector converts the information into electrical impulses that are then made audible via a digital–analog converter and a loudspeaker.

Digital music

Portable music players have even made the home stereo system redundant and they come with all kinds of accessories such as specialised loudspeakers. MP3 players can also be connected to conventional music systems and car radios.

As music is increasingly downloaded directly from the Internet fewer and fewer people are buying CDs.

This is only possible because the pieces of music have been digitised and compressed. Today, music is digitised on production. Older pieces of music had to convert the analog sound waves into digital data via a digital–analog converter. A four-minute-piece of music would have a size of 40 MB when converted and would therefore need to compressed to make it easier to handle. There are several ways of doing this. The piece could be made most compact by using 'lossy compression' techniques, but it would lose some of its sound quality.

MP3 has become the most popular digital compression format for music all over the world. The format was developed in Germany. Although using this format does result in some loss of sound quality, most people cannot detect this. The format exploits the fact that humans cannot detect sounds above a frequency of 20,000 Hertz. These sounds are therefore removed. The same is true of very low sounds. Where loud sounds are superimposed on softer sounds, the softer sounds can also be removed.

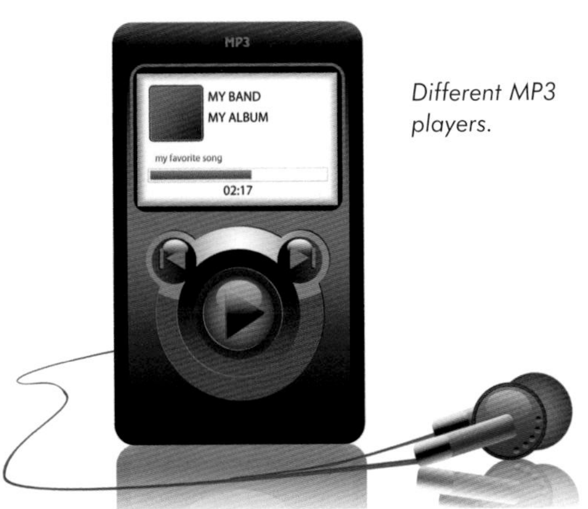

Different MP3 players.

As a result, a four-minute song can be compressed to a size of 4 MB and can easily be stored without taking up too much space.

MP3 has changed the music market: songs can now be sent and exchanged very quickly. No carrier medium is necessary and the music's sound quality is not affected. Digital music has spread uncontrollably via the Internet and songs are often downloaded without musicians receiving their royalties.

By the end of the 1990s, MP3 made music much more mobile. To use a Walkman or Discman you needed to carry several cassettes or CDs. Now you can store a huge amount of music digitally on a small MP3 player. The biggest MP3 players have integrated hard drives with enough space for entire music collections (e.g. with space for 160 GB or 40,000 songs) and even videos. Songs can be selected by turning a knob or by using a touch screen. Smaller devices store music using flash memory (a memory chip similar to ones in USB sticks) or in replaceable storage cards. Flash memory needs less energy and is more robust. The devices also include a sound chip – a circuit that converts digital data back into analog sounds. Many mobile phones now include integral MP3 players and music data can be downloaded from a PC onto the phone via a USB port.

35mm
CCD
DSP
COMPRESSED DATA
ADC
DIGITAL DATA
ANALOG DATA

CHAPTER 7

Optics

Optics is concerned with learning about and understanding the physics of light. Many inventions are based on the laws of optics. As far back as in the ancient world people were aware of the distorted images created by glass balls filled with water. Lens systems were developed in the 13th century using individual lenses, to look at small or distant objects.

Johannes Janssen, a Dutch spectacle maker, and his son Zacharias built the first telescope. In 1933 the electron microscope was developed, and further developments made it possible to have magnifications of millions of times. Telescopes were developed by the Jannssen family as well as J. Lippershey (1608). The invention of the reflecting telescope made it possible to explore the universe. The lens also has an important role in photography and film technology. Leonardo da Vinci described seeing strange light phenomena when rays of light fell into a dark room through a small hole. His observations, along with those of many others, led to the invention of the *laterna magica* or magic lantern in the middle of the 17th century, a projector that created glass transparencies. Apart from the lens, photography needed a means of exposing and developing the photographed image. Niepce and Daguerre succeeded in doing this in 1820. Today we have SLR (single-lens reflex) cameras and many kinds of compact camera, most of them digital.

Film technology developed in similar ways. The first 'living' pictures were created from a combination of several magic lantern slides. The invention of celluloid film led to the first short films in 1890 in Great Britain, films with sound followed soon after.

Lenses and light refraction

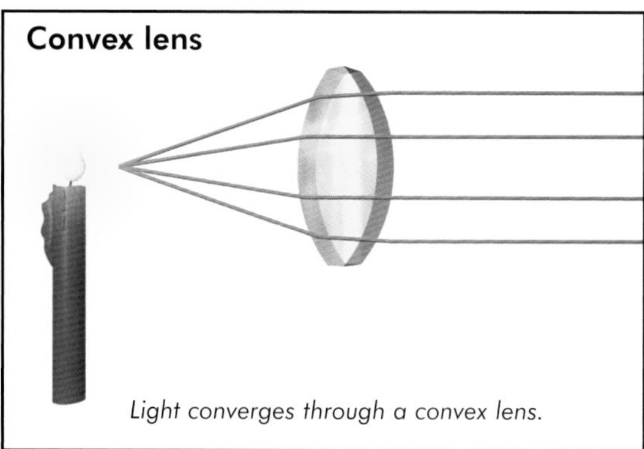
Convex lens

Light converges through a convex lens.

Developing instruments such as cameras, the microscope or the telescope required knowledge of the basics of optics, such as how lenses and light refraction works.

The lens in an optical system is a transparent object made of glass or synthetic material. When light hits the material, the light will be refracted (or redirected) in a particular direction, depending on the shape of the lens. Lenses that curve outwards are know as convex lenses. Light rays converge when they pass through a convex lens. Lenses that curve inwards are called concave lenses and, by contrast, light rays diverge through a concave lens.

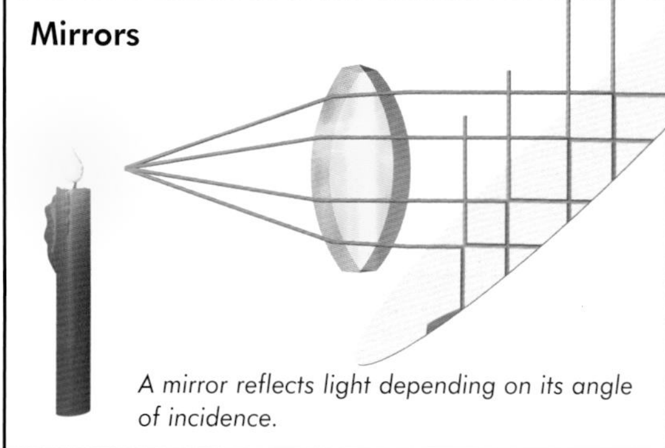
Mirrors

A mirror reflects light depending on its angle of incidence.

White light is composed of different colours of the spectrum. Its components are refracted to different degrees depending on their respective wavelengths. Therefore when light penetrates a lens, the colours are split up. Refraction can lead to different focal points forming so that a ring of colour forms around an image. When this happens it is known as chromatic aberration. Using a combination of lenses can correct the aberration. The resulting focus is the same as with one lens, but the chromatic aberration is reduced. Not all aberrations can be corrected. In the film industry only the basic colours blue, red and green need to be corrected since only these colours are used to generate images and are mixed as needed. In astronomical telescopes, however, it is essential to be able to work without chromatic aberration. Giant, curved mirrors are used to ensure this.

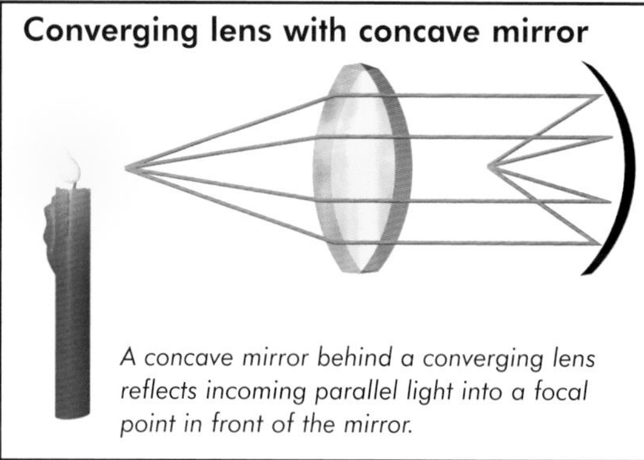
Converging lens with concave mirror

A concave mirror behind a converging lens reflects incoming parallel light into a focal point in front of the mirror.

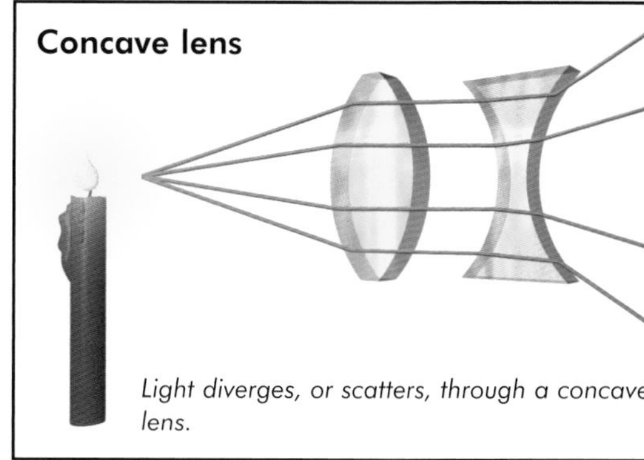
Concave lens

Light diverges, or scatters, through a concave lens.

In photography, distortions can be avoided by using a small 'aperture' so that only the light rays that hit the centre of the lens get through.

The focal length of a lens is another important feature in a lens. The focal length is the distance between the focal point of a lens and the point at which the image of a distant object is viewed.

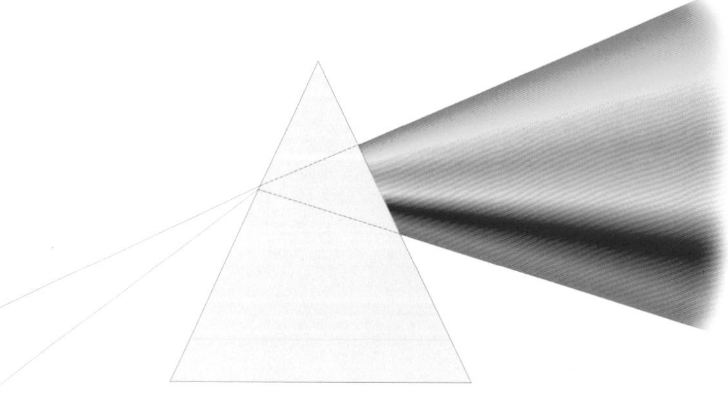
In a ***prism****, white light is refracted and broken up into its spectral colours so that the light dispersed by a prism displays the colours of the rainbow. White light is in fact a mix of all the different wavelengths of visible light. As they leave the prism the light waves of the different colours are refracted at different levels, leaving the prism at different points. This makes it possible to see the individual colours in the light spectrum. Red is refracted the least, and violet the most.*

Microscopes

Microscopes use different kinds of lens to magnify the view of small objects and substances (specimens) at a short distance in order to observe and investigate them in detail.

Hans and Zacharias Janssen probably built the first microscope in Holland in 1590. Lenses were used for magnification with something similar to a magnifying glass, before this date. Antoni van Leeuwenhoek is seen as a pioneer of microscopy. He used a hand-ground lens, which could be used to observe an object using a long adjustment screw. This very simple microscope was able to magnify images by 300 times. Modern microscopes can magnify images by 1,000 times.

Modern light microscopes have several parts, including a 'stage', an illuminator, optical systems and a base. The optical systems have several 'objectives', which are housed in a 'revolving nosepiece'. The objectives create magnified images. The size of the image can be adjusted by using different objectives. A prepared specimen is placed on a slide and covered with a coverslip. It can then be viewed through the eyepiece or 'ocular'. An intermediate image is produced which is then viewed through the ocular at a higher magnification. To calculate the total magnification of the object, the magnification of the objective has to be multiplied by the magnification of the ocular. A magnification of 10 through the ocular and of 20 through the objective produces a total magnification of 200 times for the viewer. The light needed for microscopy is reflected through an

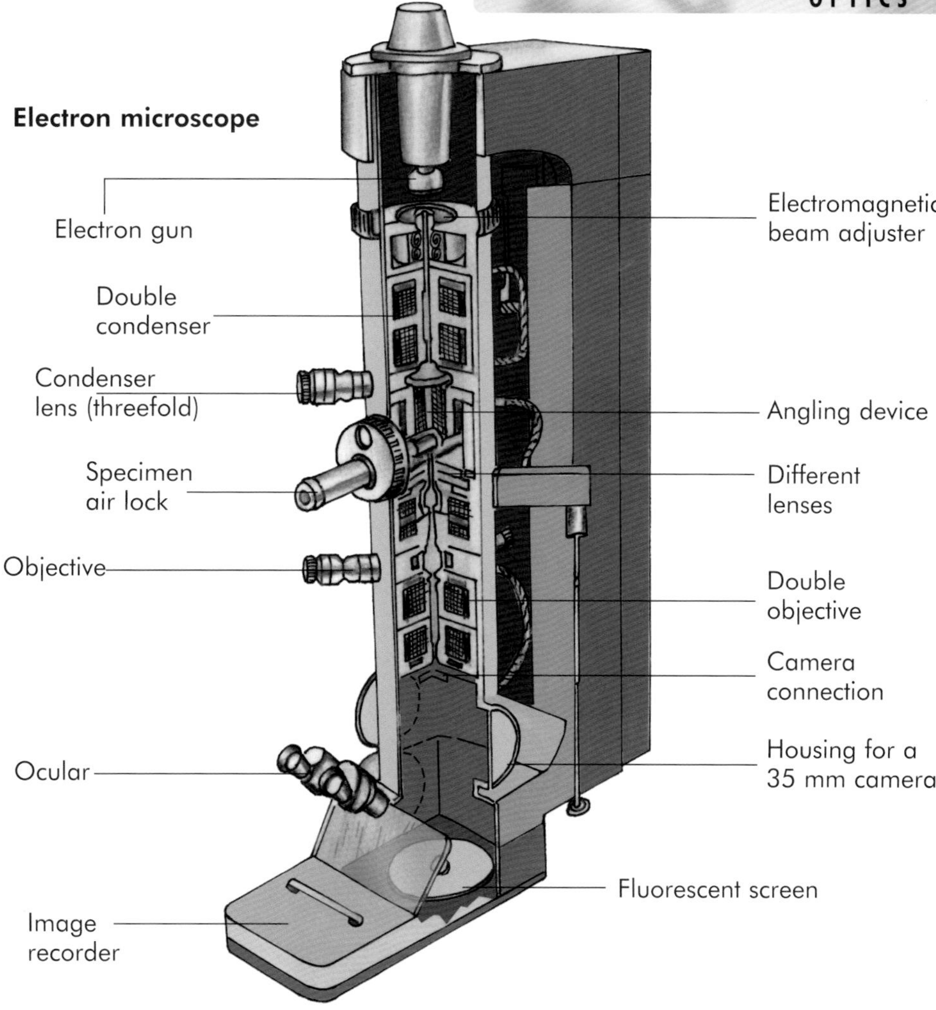

How a light microscope works
A microscope makes it possible to see things that are invisible to the naked eye. A specimen that is as thin and as transparent as possible is placed on a slide that is placed on the stage of a microscope. The light needed is then directed from below to penetrate through the specimen and into the lens in the ocular. Modern light microscopes use different objectives housed within a revolving nosepiece. The level of magnification (higher or lower) can be changed by using different objectives. The biggest magnification possible using a light microscope is about x1,500.

illuminating mirror below the objective. The light is beamed from below and then through the specimen and lens to the eye of the viewer.

Magnifications of 100,000 times are possible with an electron microscope. These devices work with electrons whose beams are considerably finer than light waves. Magnifications of as much as a hundred million times are possible with a 'tunnel microscope'.

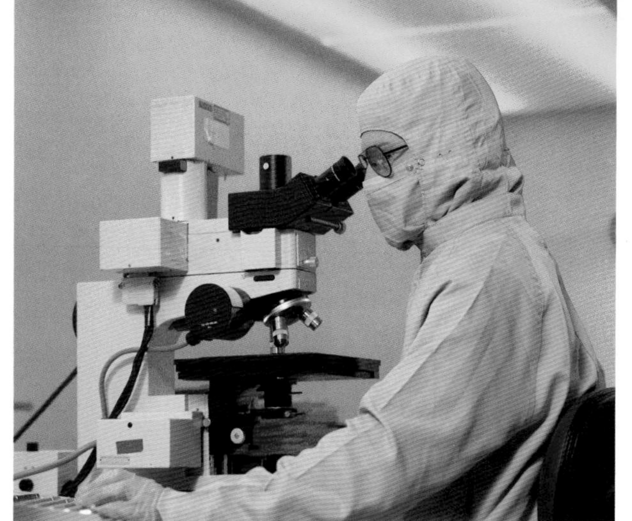

Electron microscope

Telescopes

Telescope

Telescopes use prisms, lenses and mirrors to make things that are very far away appear closer to us.

In 1608 the Dutch spectacle maker Lippershey built one of the first diopter telescopes using two lenses. Galileo Galilei had heard of the telescope and in 1609 built a long telescope, which he could use for astronomical observations. Various kinds of telescope with differently shaped lenses and mirrors were developed over the next few centuries.

There are two main types of telescope today: refracting and reflecting telescopes. Every refracting telescope consists of an objective that is directed at the observed image and an ocular that is placed against the eye. The light waves being emitted from the observed image enter the objective parallel to each other and then converge on a focal point. The ocular has a focal point at exactly the same place so that the waves also exit the ocular in parallel formation. The observed object appears as a magnified image.

In a Galilean telescope, the objective has a convex lens and the ocular a concave one. The distance between the two is the difference between their focal points. The viewer sees an upright image. This kind of telescope is used for hunting or in opera glasses with low magnification.

A Keplerian telescope has convex lenses for both the objective and ocular, producing an upside-down image. This is not problematic for astronomical observation; a further

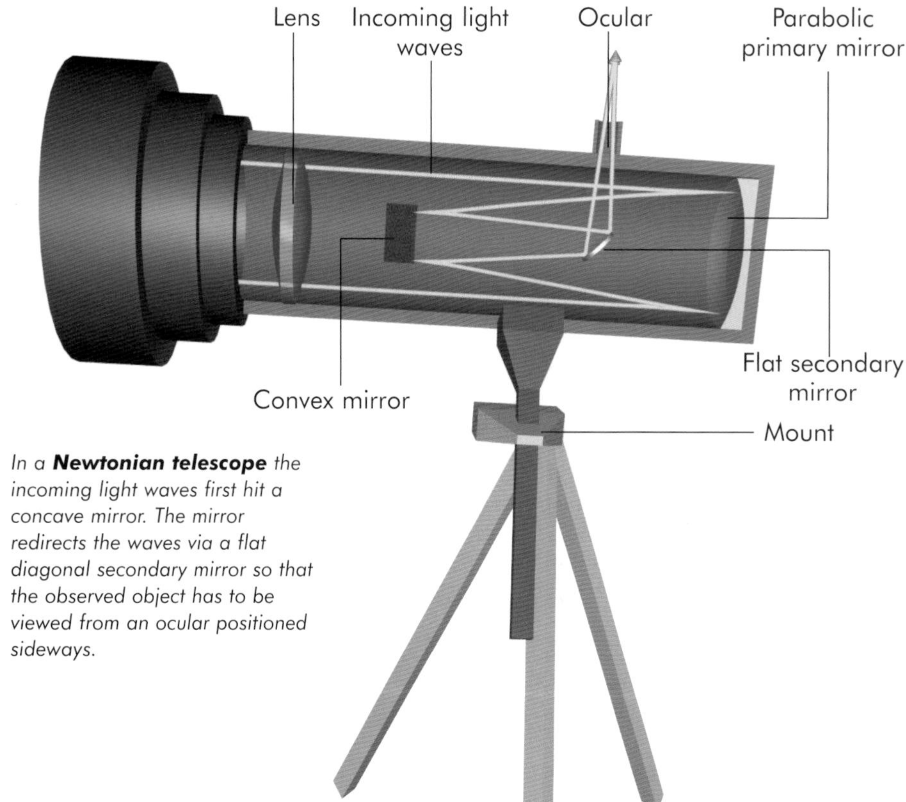

*In a **Newtonian telescope** the incoming light waves first hit a concave mirror. The mirror redirects the waves via a flat diagonal secondary mirror so that the observed object has to be viewed from an ocular positioned sideways.*

Telescopes have been around since the 16th century. The primary purpose of a telescope is to create a magnified retinal image of an object by increasing the viewer's angle of vision. A telescope consists of a long tube, a convex lens with a long focal length, an objective and an ocular that is used like a magnifying glass. Telescopes have been used for sky watching since Galileo's time. Refracting telescopes use convex lenses as objectives. The convex lens creates an upside-down image at a set distance according to the focal length of the lens. Viewed through the ocular the image appears greatly magnified. The light waves penetrate the telescope in parallel and meet at the focal point. The ocular is positioned at a set distance from the focal point. A telescope does not magnify an image but makes an observed object appear to be closer to the viewer than it really is.

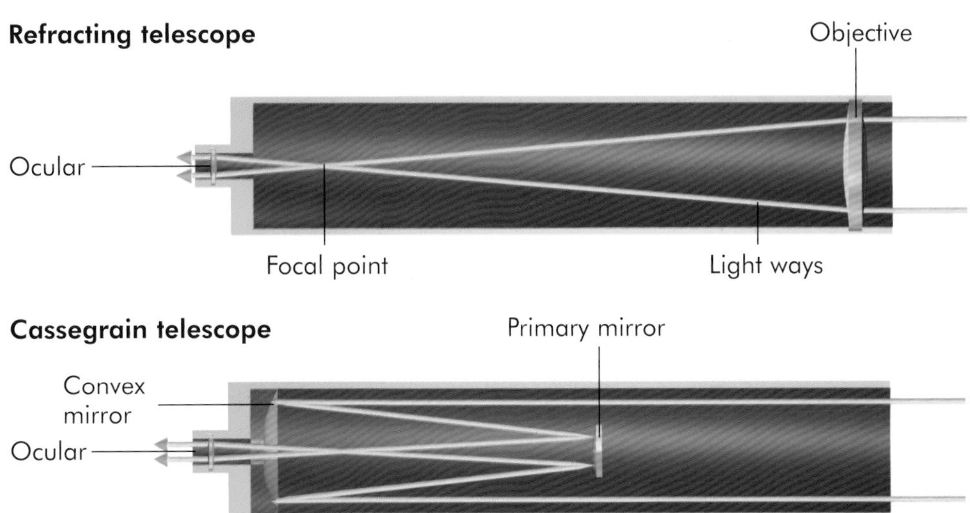

convex lens is added to correct the image when used for observation on earth.

There are two kinds of reflecting telescope: the Newtonian and Cassegrain telescopes. Both use one concave mirror. In a Newtonian telescope the parallel incoming waves of an object hit a concave mirror and are redirected via a secondary diagonal flat mirror to an ocular positioned on one side. The mirror directs the focal point to the ocular. In a Cassegrain telescope the secondary mirror is convex and positioned in such a way that the waves only converge to form an image once they have passed through a hole in the middle of the primary mirror.

Several giant reflecting telescopes with mirrors with a diametre of 2 metres have been erected in various places around the world over the last few years. Examples are the reflecting telescope of the Mount Palomar Observatory in California and the Keck Telescope in Mauna Kea (Hawaii).

Radio telescope

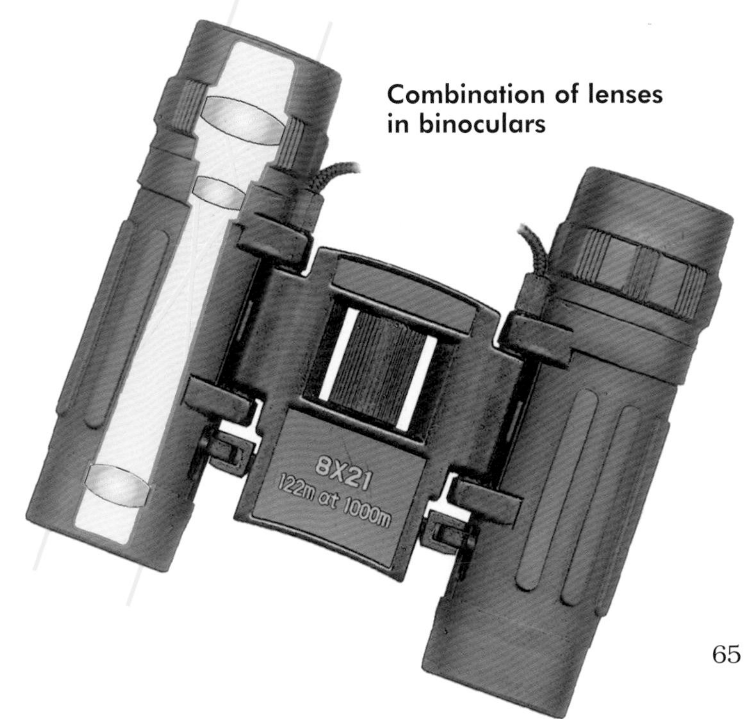

Combination of lenses in binoculars

Photography

The development of photography made it possible to take long-lasting and realistic images of people and objects in the world.

Several past inventors made significant contributions to the development of photography. In 1826 Joseph Niepce took one of the earliest photographs. It was of a landscape and still exists. He used a 'camera obscura' and a light-sensitive zinc plate. He needed eight hours to obtain sufficient exposure. At about the same time L. J. M. Daguerre started experimenting with iodised layers of silver on copper plates. They worked together to further develop the first usable photographic process, known as Daguerreotype. In this process silver-plated plates treated with iodine fumes were developed and fixed by using mercury fumes after exposure. Although an image was created it could not be reproduced. The British inventor William H. F. Talbot succeeded in developing what is still known as the negative–positive method of photography.

By the end of the 19th century, the early light-sensitive metal plates

Taking a photograph with a magnesium flash light in Birmingham around 1860

A darkroom

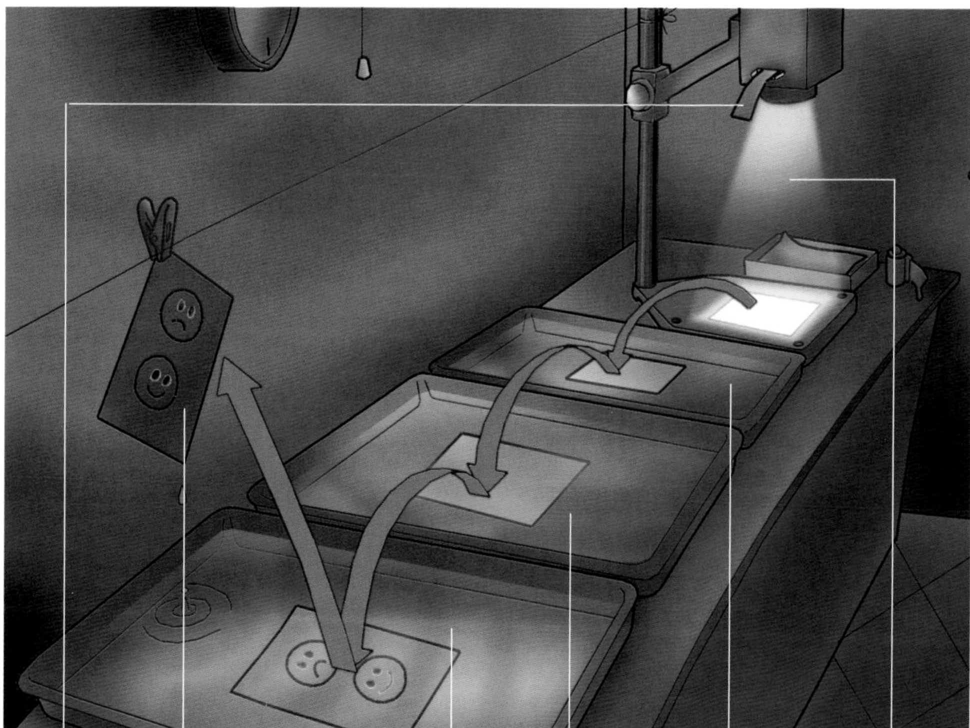

*In **analog photography**, unlike in digital photography, various chemical processes are used to get the finished photo. The negative image is projected onto light-sensitive paper, which results in a positive image after being developed in a bath of developer. The image is then placed in a 'stop bath' and the chemical process ends with a bath in fixative. After being soaked and dried once more the photo is ready.*

Modern photography
William Henry Fox Talbot, a British inventor, developed the negative–positive method in 1839. The process made it possible to have multiple copies of a photo. This was an important step towards modern photography.

had evolved into rolls of film.

In order to record an image, a camera, consisting of a box, objective and shutter release, has to capture the chosen framed image onto a light-sensitive medium. In traditional photography the medium used is film. Film undergoes chemical changes when exposed to light, thereby recording an image. In digital photography, the light is focused onto a light-sensitive image sensor.

In analog photography the differences in brightness are recorded by one or more light-sensitive layers. For black-and-white photographs only one layer is used. The image collected is invisible at this stage of the process. To develop a film it has to be placed in a liquid bath of developer for a specific amount of time. It then has to be fixed in a saline solution. This process creates a 'negative' which can be converted into a positive image and even magnified by following yet another process.

A negative image projected onto photographic paper results in a positive image. The negatives remain unchanged and can be used to make numerous copies of the photographs, in different sizes. Today, digital cameras are used almost exclusively, with compact cameras used for amateur photography and reflex cameras for professional use.

Folding camera with bellows

The oldest portrait by John Draper

Analog and digital cameras

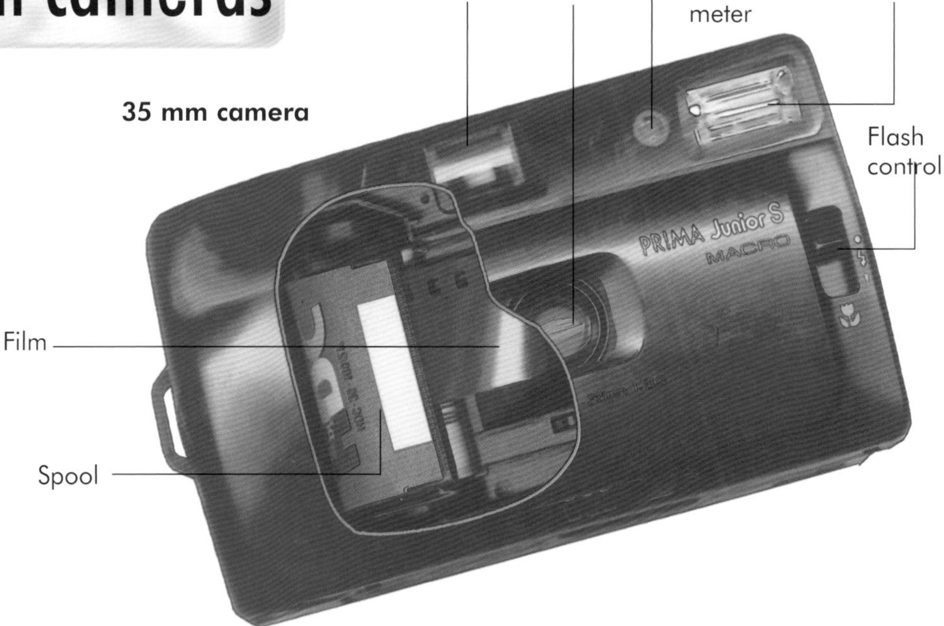

The early years of photography (in the time of Daguerre and Niepce) were arduous for both photographer and subject. The equipment was large and awkward to operate; the long exposure time involved sitting still patiently to ensure a successful photo.

By the time of the invention of the first film rolls in 1898 exposure times had been significantly reduced. Exposure time is the amount of time during which a film is exposed to light. The time could be reduced to a fraction of a second in bright conditions, when a very short exposure is needed. In faint light a longer exposure is still needed. A shutter release was developed to set exposure time, and an aperture determined the amount of light that was let in. Several decades ago these adjustments had to be made manually and were extremely complicated.

A modern camera consists of a lens, aperture, shutter release and lightproof housing. The lens is right at the front of the camera and is in fact made up of several optical lenses. This makes it possible to focus directly on the subject being photographed to obtain a sharp image on the film or image sensor. The aperture and shutter release are coordinated and ensure the right amount of light is allowed in. The shorter the exposure time the wider the aperture needed in order to maintain the same quantity of light. The aperture is a round, adjustable opening. The smaller the aperture value setting on a camera the wider the aperture opening will be. A small aperture opening will result in a large depth of field where even distant objects in a picture will be clearly identifiable. The shutter release which regulates the amount of light, and hence exposure time, is right inside the camera's optical path. In cameras today the aperture opening and exposure time are usually controlled by an automatic exposure mechanism inside the camera. A viewfinder makes it easy to select the image you want to photograph.

Camera controls are automated today. Exposure, shutter release and many other functions from focusing to automatic detection of a smile are all automatically regulated through the electronic systems installed in the camera.

The first digital cameras for domestic consumers became available in the 1990s and were

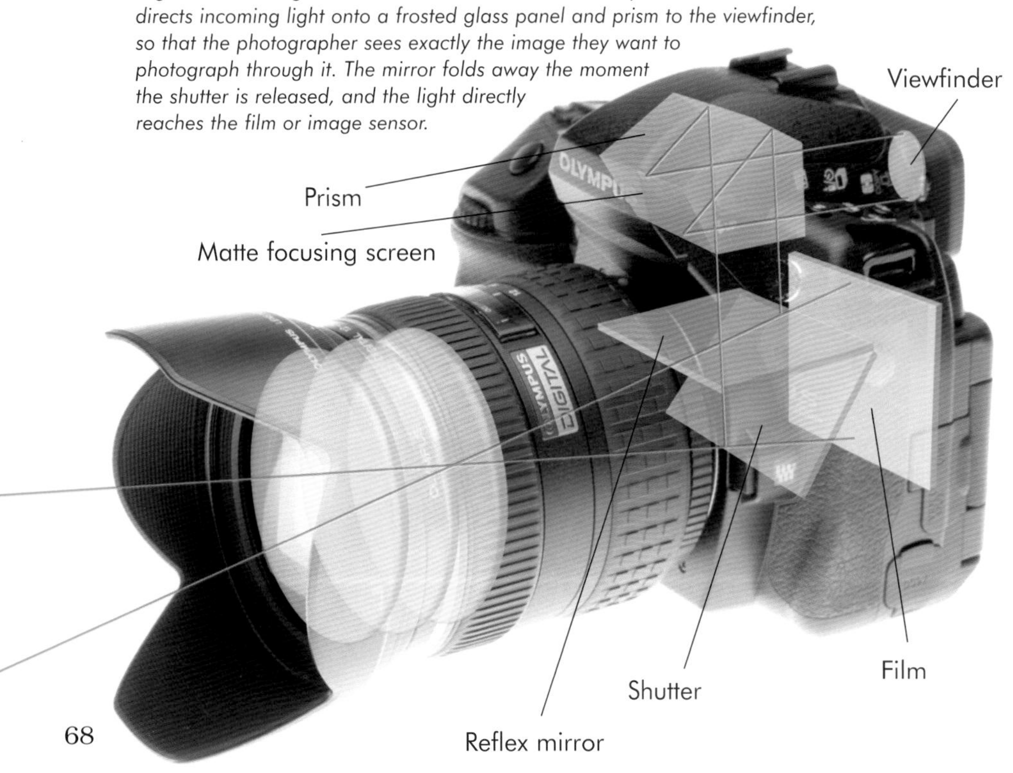

Digital and analog SLR cameras both have an inbuilt, dynamic mirror that directs incoming light onto a frosted glass panel and prism to the viewfinder, so that the photographer sees exactly the image they want to photograph through it. The mirror folds away the moment the shutter is released, and the light directly reaches the film or image sensor.

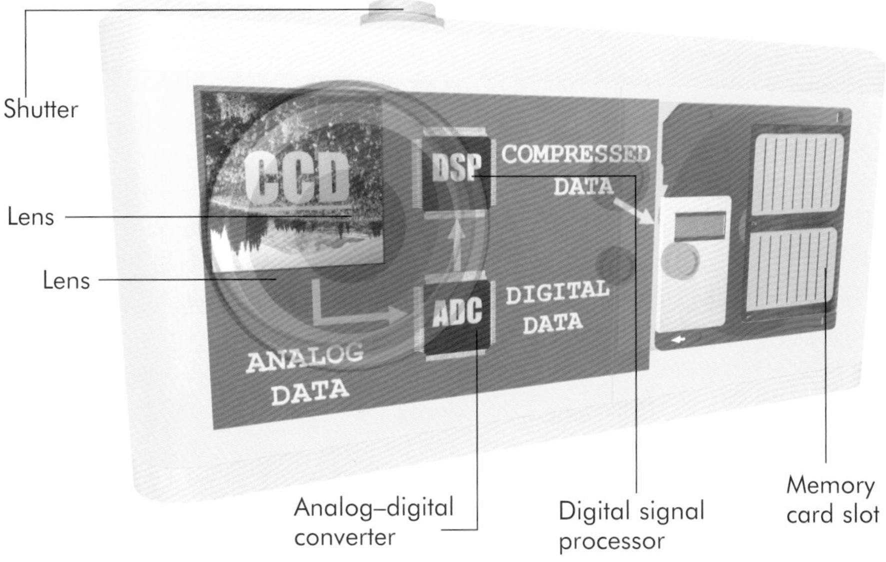

As in a conventional camera, in digital cameras light enters the camera through the lens. The light is focused on a component made up of light detectors (transistors), which react to the strength and brightness of the light (a CCD chip). The CCD chip converts the light into electrical charges and an analog–digital converter (ADC) turns the electrons into digital image signals. These are then transported to the memory card via the signal processor.

Digital reflex cameras usually have both a viewfinder and a display panel, while compact digital cameras usually only have a display panel.

enthusiastically received. They have many advantages: you can see the photos you have taken immediately on the display; you don't have to limit yourself to 24 or 36 photos per film roll; you can delete photos immediately, store them and send them to others easily.

As in an analog camera, light enters the camera through the lens. Everything else is different, however: the image sensor that the light hits is made up of multiple pixels. The number of pixels is expressed in megapixels. The more megapixels a camera has the higher the resolution of the photos. (A high number of megapixels does not automatically mean a camera is better, however; the quality of a camera also depends on other things such as the size of the sensor.) An image sensor measures the intensity of light and uses a filter to determine the brightness of the green, blue and red colour elements of the light spectrum. All this information is then turned into digital signals, compressed and stored in the storage device, which is usually a memory card. Compact cameras are the most common kind of camera. They often have an automatic zoom, and hence the possibility of setting different focal lengths in order to enlarge an image. It is also possible to record video with most compact cameras. Most mobile phones have inbuilt cameras for taking photos and videos as well.

A typical compact digital camera with extended zoom.

Film technology

The development of film technology made it possible to create moving pictures. Taking a film involves taking a rapid series of individual static photos.

Old-fashioned film projector

Film technology had its beginnings in the 18th century in the *laterna magica* or 'magic lantern', which projected the first silhouettes of writing and images onto a wall. In 1830 individual animated slides were shown and 15 years later a 'living wheel' of moving pictures was projected with the magic lantern. In 1891 Thomas A. Edison obtained a patent for his 'kinetoscope'. It made use of celluloid filmstrips, an electric motor and a light bulb as its light source. Five years later the brothers Auguste and Louis Lumière showed the first silent movie to the general public. In subsequent years film technology developed steadily in terms of editing, animation and shooting, but the real basis of modern cinema was only established with the invention of sound films in 1926. The representation of motion in film is based on the particular properties of the human eye. When an image is transferred from the lens to the retina, the brain receives nerve signals from the retina. This continues for a short while even after the image has been removed from view, especially when there is poor lighting (known as dark adaptation). If a series of pictures is shown within a short enough time frame, our eyes merge them together and the impression of continuous movement is created. Films make use of this principle. A film camera shoots several pictures within a second. The film roll used to do this has to move correspondingly quickly. In order to take 24 pictures in a second (the usual rate at which film cameras operate), you would need twenty-seven metres of 35mm film (small film camera) to run through the camera per minute. This is why film cameras are equipped with substantial film-holding capacity. While the film has to roll at speed it also has to move sufficiently slowly to capture enough light for the pictures. The film is guided over special sprocket wheels with teeth, which hold the

Film reels

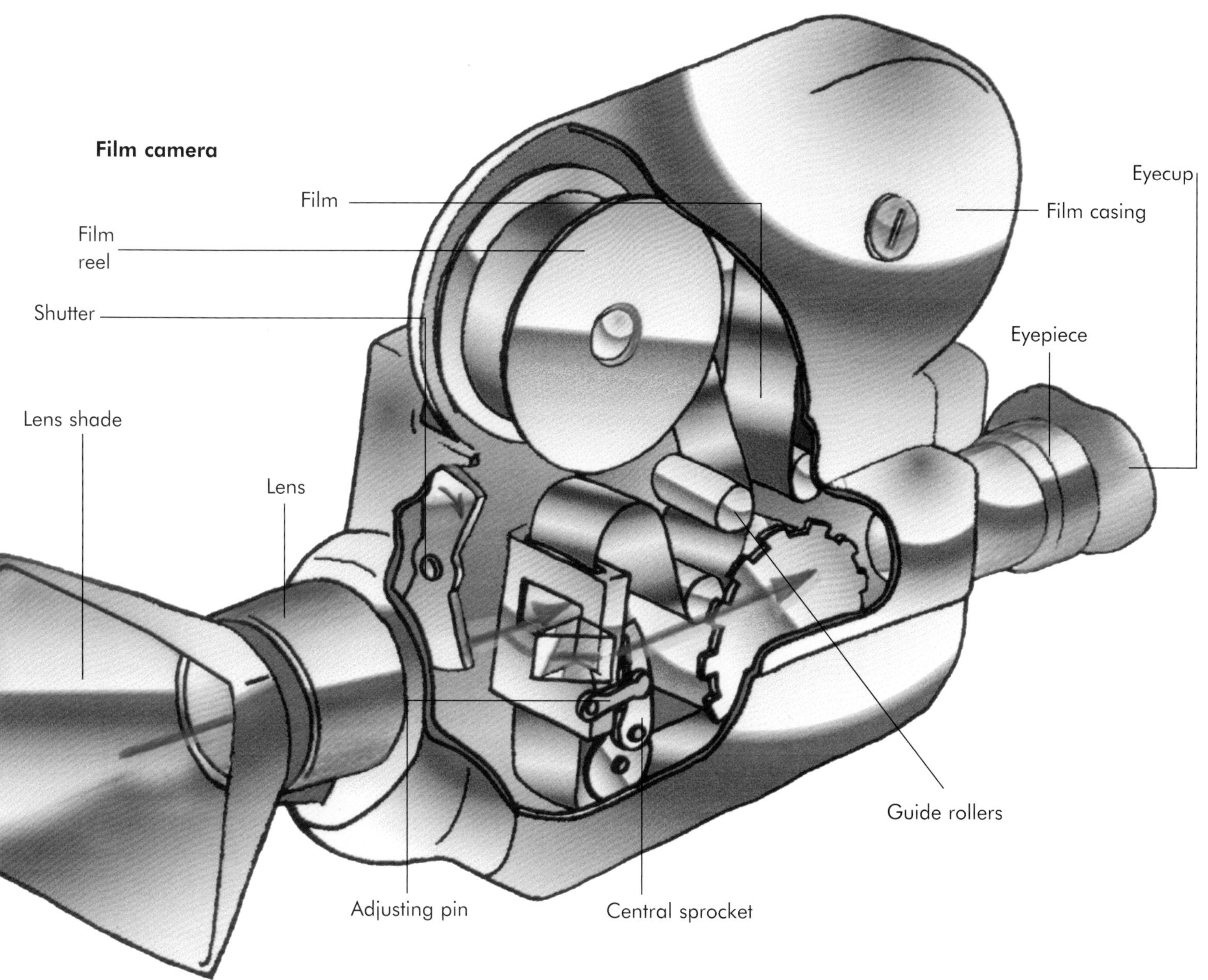

perforated edges of the film. Every picture 'frame' passes through an 'image window'. A lens in front of the shutter of the image window focuses on the image of the scene being filmed. A rotating shutter between the lens and film rotates constantly, opening to expose every frame and closing just as a new frame appears. A special mechanism moves the film reel on while holding it in place for each frame exposure. Once a sequence has been filmed a machine develops the negative film and a printer (e.g. a contact copier) turns the negative film into a positive film. If the film and its sound and speech have to be synchronised the sound is recorded during filming. Specialised 'sync' cameras are used for this purpose. Sound can also be recorded separately on magnetic tape and then mixed and synchronised with the film after recording. Today, filming is almost exclusively done with digital cameras and then finished on computers.

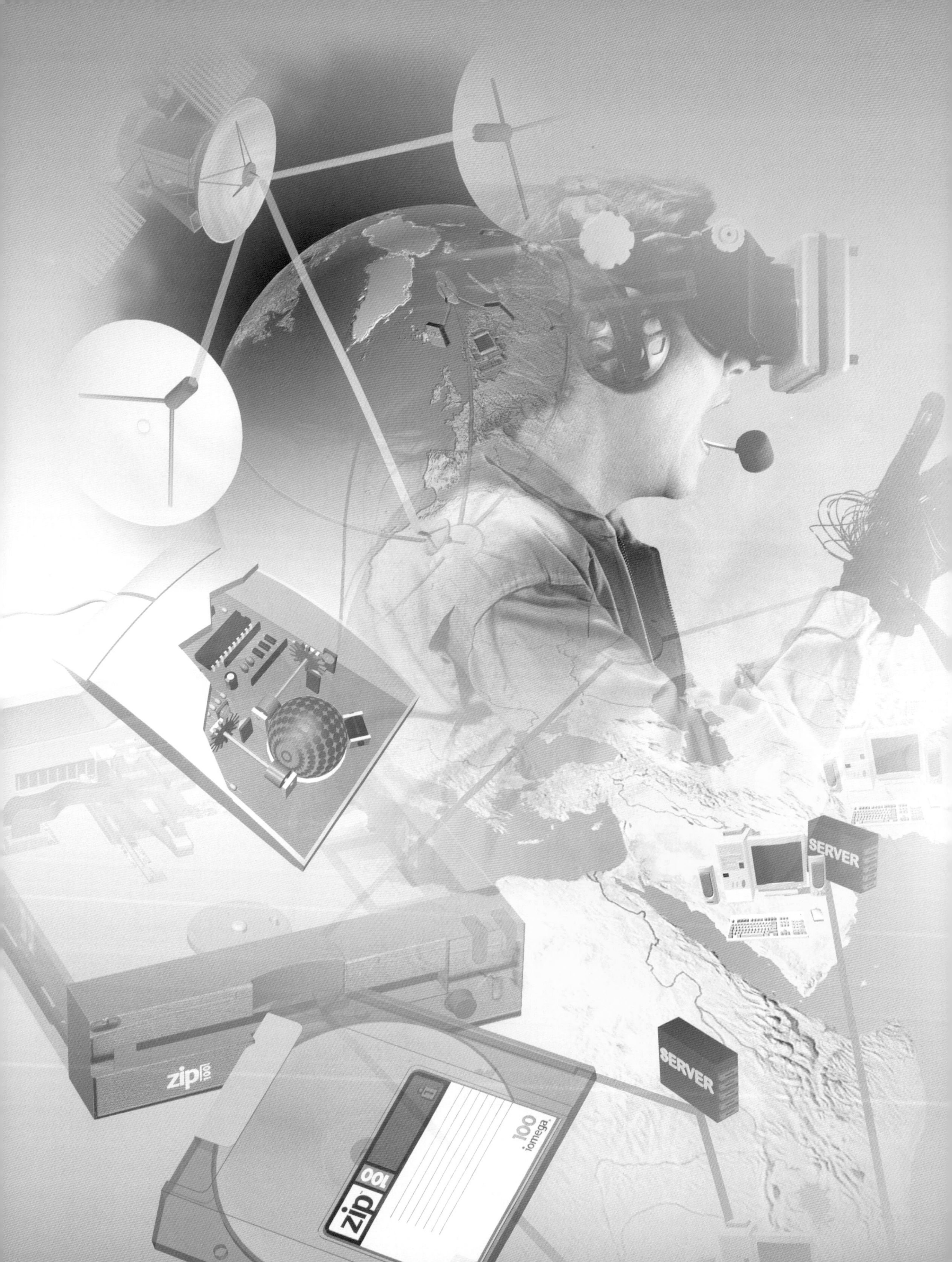
SERVER
zip
SERVER
100
iomega
zip
100

CHAPTER 8

Computers

When we use the word 'computer' today, we usually mean a PC, a personal computer. However, from autopilots in aeroplanes to bookkeeping, there are few areas of modern life where we don't use computers. In private homes, computers are used for personal pastimes (games, learning, organising music collections), communication (e-mail and social networking) and obtaining information (via the Internet).

The basic idea of mechanising the solving of arithmetical problems existed in the ancient world in the form an abacus. Punch cards were developed in 1800, using simple binary codes, and were the first step towards the modern computer. They were gradually replaced by electronic mechanisms. The first relay computer was the ZI invented by K. Zuse in 1937. Transistors, and eventually chips with integrated circuits, were the prerequisites of the modern compact PC. The components became smaller and smaller so that the technology needed for a modern computer today fits not just into a desktop but also into a portable computer such as a notebook, netbook or tablet, or indeed into a mobile phone.

Bits and bytes

The binary system
The decimal 87 converted into a binary code:

1 0 1 0 1 1 1

87/2 = 43 remainder 1
43/2 = 21 remainder 1
21/2 = 10 remainder 1
10/2 = 5 remainder 0
5/2 = 2 remainder 1
2/2 = 1 remainder 0
1/2 = 0 remainder 1

Decimal number	Binary number
0	00000
1	00001
2	00010
3	00011
4	00100
5	00101
6	00110
7	00111
8	01000
9	01001
10	01010
11	01011
12	01100

Bits are the smallest units of information that a computer can process. A byte is a made up of eight bits.

In computers, information is represented by the presence or absence of electrical current. A binary code is used to do this: a computer uses two digits to represent 'yes' and 'no' to express everything else. Any information can be coded and encoded using a binary code.

'Bit' is short for Binary Digit. A bit can be either 1 (yes) or 0 (no). A byte, made up of a combination eight bits, can be used to represent a letter of the alphabet, a number or a punctuation mark. The various possible combinations of binary digits can create a total 256 different signs. So, for example, the letter 'A' is created by the combination 01000001. All the letters of the alphabet and digits from 0 to 9 can be represented in this way. The next biggest single unit made up of bits is a kilobyte (KB). A kilobyte is 1,024 bits. A megabyte is 1,048,576 bits.

The standard code that translates every character from a computer keyboard into a digit is known as ASCII. There is a different set of ASCII digits for every single letter of the alphabet, written in lower or upper case. If you press the letter 'm' on a keyboard this information will be converted into its binary value of the ASCII code. The letter 'm' has the value 109 and the electrical code 01101101, which is communicated to the computer. ASCII cannot represent all the characters used in the world, so Unicode, which uses 32 bits for a character, was developed.

The sizes of a hard disk, main memory or external memory media are also expressed in bytes. Early PCs had only a 10 MB memory storage capacity (a megabyte is 1,024 kilobytes or 1,048,576 bytes). Since 1997 memory size has been expressed in GB or gigabytes (a gigabyte is 1,073,741,824 bytes, so over a billion bytes) or even in TB, terabytes (a terabyte is 1,024 gigabytes).

A motherboard

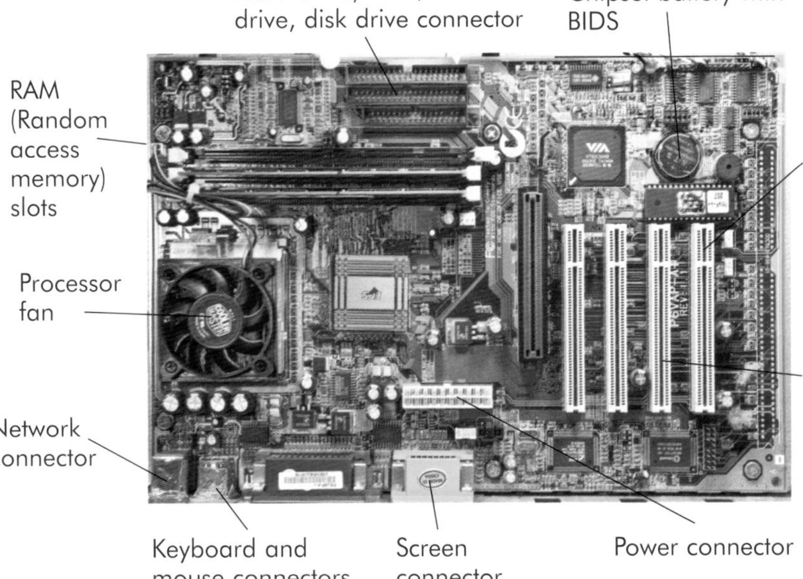

Keyboard

Mouse

When you strike a key on a keyboard, the current flow in a connected wire is changed. The keyboard processor checks for multiple changes in voltage in the keyboard circuitry at the rate of 100 changes per second. When the processor registers a key being pressed the relevant code is transmitted to a 'keyboard buffer'. A signal is also sent to the keyboard control chip within the keyboard. The control chip sends the signal on to the PC. This signal, known as 'interrupt' tells the computer that it is going to get information from the keyboard. The central processor unit (CPU) kick-starts the reading of the keyboard codes in the keyboard buffer and deciphers which keys have been operated using the keyboard driver and the BIOS (basic input/output system) located in the computer's RAM (random access memory). Following this, a corresponding code will be written in the keyboard buffer of the RAM, which is then read as needed.

Central processors

The processor, also known as the central processing unit (CPU), is the heart of every computer. This is where all the data and computer processing is done. The CPU is made up of several building blocks, which in modern PCs are all contained on a microchip, hence the term 'microprocessor'.

The processor has an in-built arithmetic logic unit, which drives the processing of logic and arithmetic operations such as data linking. Program and input/output control commands are converted into circuits here with the resulting signals sent out to the internal (main memory) and external (external storage device) units of the computer. The data, instructions and results needed to execute a function are briefly stored in the computer's main memory. A control unit regulates the order in which tasks are carried out, although today's computers can perform several tasks at once. The control unit decodes commands and transmits the signals (logical connections or postponements) needed to perform a task to the relevant arithmetic logic unit. The CPU and other internal components of a computer are connected to the motherboard via a communication system called a 'bus'. An external bus connects the motherboard with peripheral devices via computer interfaces.

A microprocessor in position on a motherboard.

A fan being placed on a processor. The air cooling system (water cooling systems also exist) is necessary because processors get very hot when they are running and can overheat. In a worst-case scnenario, overheating could destroy the chip. The noise heard when a computer is running comes from the fan.

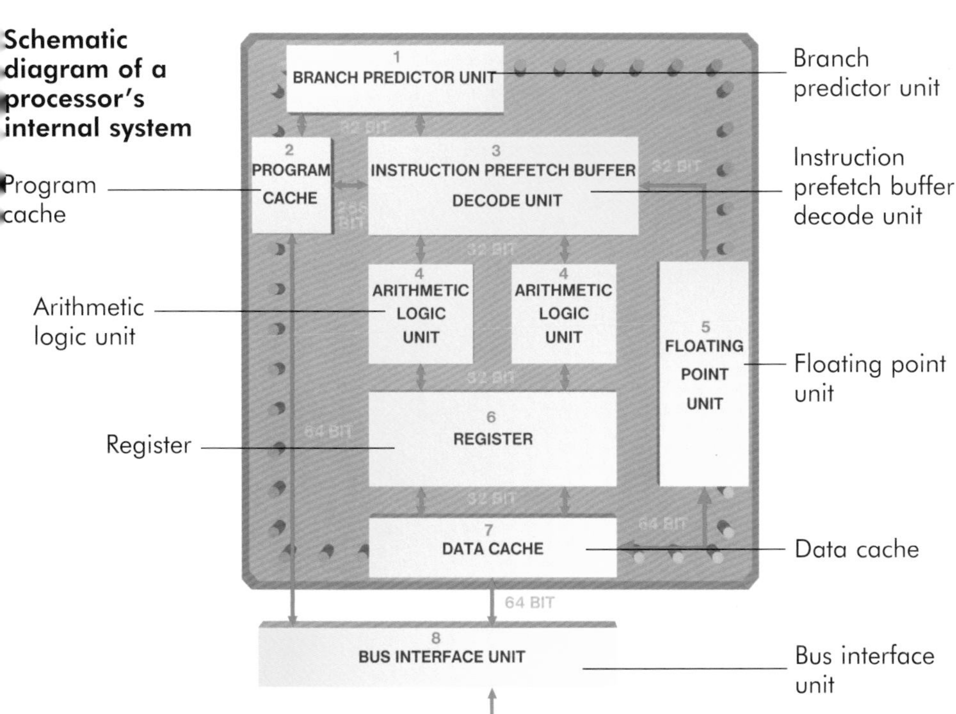

Schematic diagram of a processor's internal system

__Microchips__ are the smallest building blocks that are capable of housing a huge range of circuit components (transistors, diodes, condensers, resistors). They are made of silicon and have tiny wire nails. The wire nails can be used to create electric connections by plugging or soldering them into specific sockets.

Storage media

Typical RAM module.
The capacity of the RAM lies in individual chips (in this example they are in the form of a kind of code), multiplied by the number of chips installed – this example has eight.

Storage media are functional units used to store data internally or externally. The most important internal storage media and systems are RAM (random access memory), ROM (read only memory) and a computer's hard disk drive (HDD). Even though a hard drive is not built into the central unit of a computer, it is housed inside the computer. The RAM only stores programs and data while the computer is processing them. Once a computer is switched off the data disappear. The ROM, on the other hand, holds the computer's master data essential to its functioning. The data remain even when a computer is switched off. The hard disk drive holds all the long-term programs and data that the user stores on it.

Numerous external storage media are now available and their storage capacity seems to keep increasing. These devices can store data outside a computer that can then be accessed and used in other places on other computers.

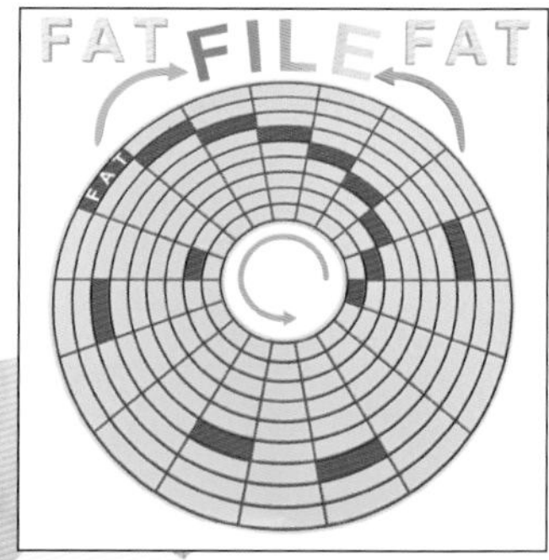

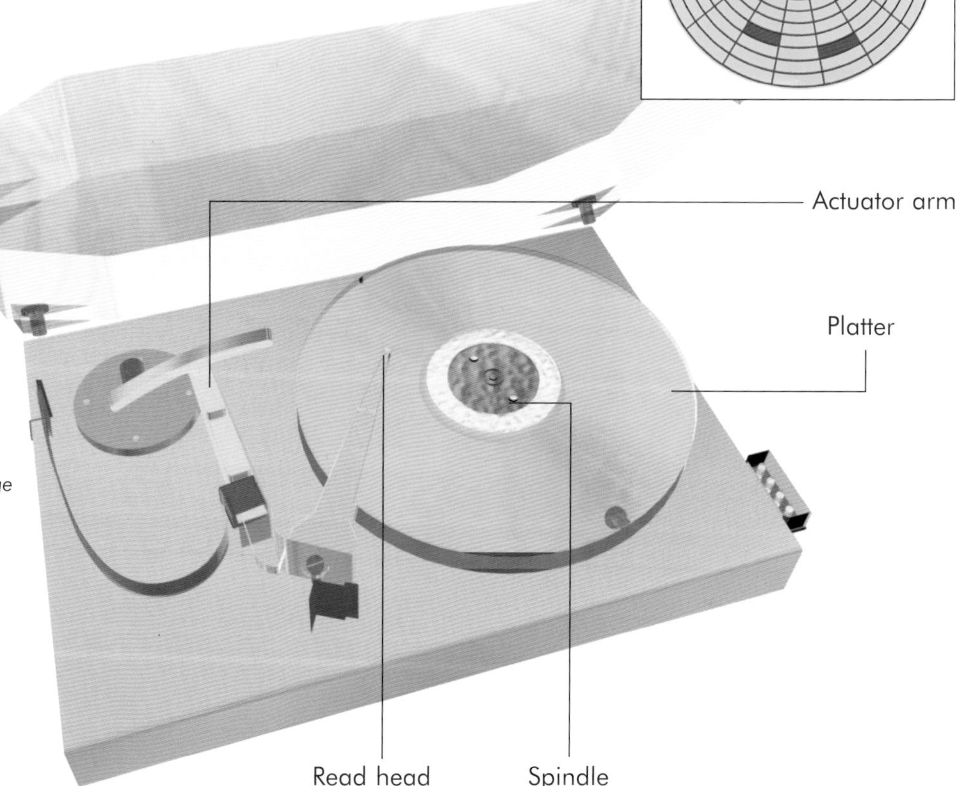

How a hard disk drive works
The hard disk is a round, magnetically coated disk or platter with concentric tracks. A read/write head flies above the disk, separated from it by an air cushion a few micrometres thick, while the disk rotates at a fixed speed. Information is stored in domains on the disk. A special domain on the edge of the disk holds the FAT or File Allocation Table. This is like the contents page of the hard disk, and holds the exact locations of all the stored data.

Data storage devices such as floppy disks with a 3.4 MB capacity that need their own drives are now hardly used in Europe.

Separate drives are also needed for CDs and DVDs with capacities of around 700 MB and 4.7-8.5 GB, although the drives for them are included in most PCs. Data can be stored on them using a disc burner.

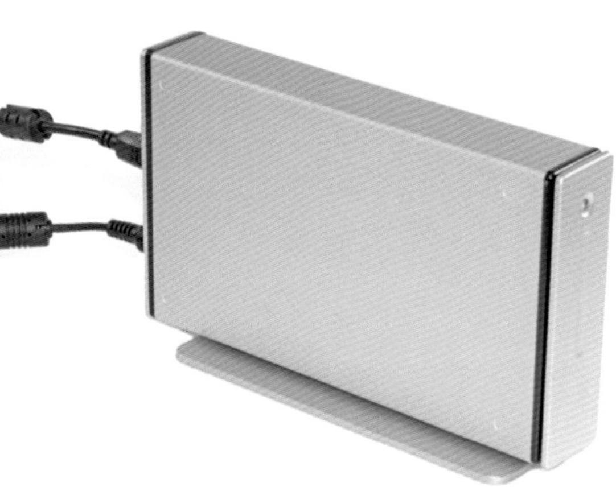

USB ports make it possible to connect external hard drives to a computer. They have a very large storage capacity so they are often used for large data files such as complete databases or films. USB sticks can be slotted into USB ports.They are practical for quickly backing up and transporting data. They are so small they fit into a trouser pocket but can also easily be lost.

Another flexible storage device is the storage card, available in different formats, for example: SD cards, CF cards, MMC cards, xD cards. They are mostly used to store data in digital cameras or mobile phones. The data can be transferred to a computer or directly to a printer or TV via a card slot.

In cloud computing a user's data isn't stored in a personal storage medium but are uploaded onto the Internet. The data is stored on a computer on the server of the cloud-computing provider. The data can be accessed at ay time via the Internet, which means the user can use any computer or mobile device to do so, even if they are in an Internet café somewhere in India. Entire programs and processes and not just data can also be stored on the Internet. Questions remain, however, about how safe such files are from access by third parties.

Notebooks, netbooks, tablets

Since the beginning of this millennium, one thing has become increasingly important for computer users: mobility. It may well be that this wasn't the driver behind decisive improvements in computer technology but the result: the improvements made mobility easier.

The first notebooks, also known as laptops, appeared in the 1980s. These portable computers with integrated screens have the same components as a desktop, but since their housing is smaller some elements needed to be removed. Since notebooks have to be light and able to operate for a length of time without being plugged in to the mains (and instead rely on a battery), and since they also have no space for large cooling systems, they cannot have built-in, energy-hungry processors or graphic cards, for example. All the components of a laptop, whether it's the hard drive or sound card, have to be smaller than in a desktop.

Despite having an externally connected mouse, notebooks also have touchpads with which the cursor on the screen can be manipulated.

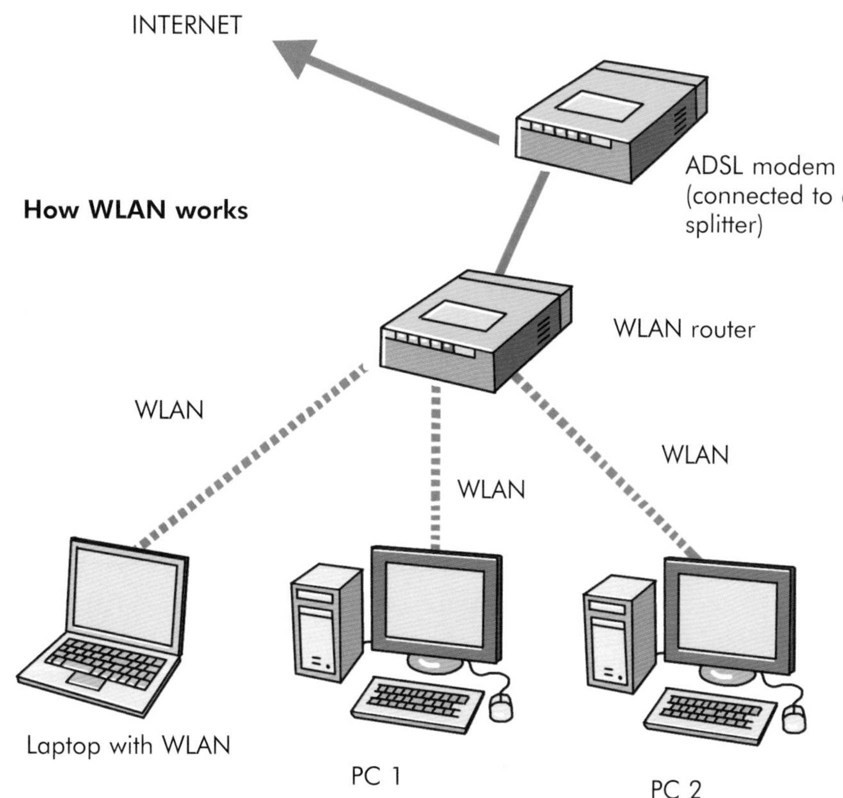

Modern notebooks are nonetheless now on a par with desktop PCs in terms of normal use. As a result, many people no longer have 'large' PCs – 70% of domestic computer users now use notebooks.

Greater mobility is now also possible because you don't have to use cables for an Internet connection. A WLAN (wireless local area network) connection makes cable-free Internet access possible in domestic and public spaces. An access point – a router that sends and receives radio signals – is needed to transmit the data from all computers (and other devices) connected to a network. Since most networks are locked, a password is needed to access to the network. Routers have a range of about 30–90 metres.

Netbooks are a smaller version of notebooks. They are used for simple tasks and mainly for mobile Internet access. They therefore have weaker processors and also no CD or DVD

As you can see, a netbook is much smaller than a notebook.

drives. Instead they have integrated WLAN and mobile communication modems to secure Internet access from WLAN hotspots while on the move.

The other type of portable computer that has rapidly become popular is the 'tablet'. These devices are extremely light and thin and their main function is to have mobile Internet access, watch films and listen to music and other similar things while on the move. The hardware and software of tablet computers have more in common with those of smartphones than with those of PCs.

Tablets do not even have keyboards and instead make use of touchscreen technology. All instruction inputs are made using fingertips directly onto a screen that covers the entire surface of the computer. There are two kinds of touchscreen: resistive and capacitive. In a resistive touchscreen, there is resistance the moment you touch the screen with your finger (even if you don't notice): one electrically conductive layer is being pressed on another such layer, so a brief contact is made. The electric resistance is measured and the location of the point at which pressure has been applied is relayed. Most tablet computers and smartphones use capacitive touchscreens, however. A constant electric field moving out from the corners of the screen covers the entire surface. The moment your finger, which also conducts electricity (but only if you aren't wearing gloves), approaches the field, there is a change in the field and a pulse is generated. A sensor detects the location of the pulse. Multi-touch control is possible in a capacitive touchscreen; this means the screen doesn't only respond to a single touch but several simultaneous ones. This makes it possible to enlarge a screen using two fingers, for example.

If a keyboard is needed this appears on the touchscreen of a tablet computer.

A typical tablet computer

On this mobile touchscreen you can clearly see the current routing network.

Peripheral devices

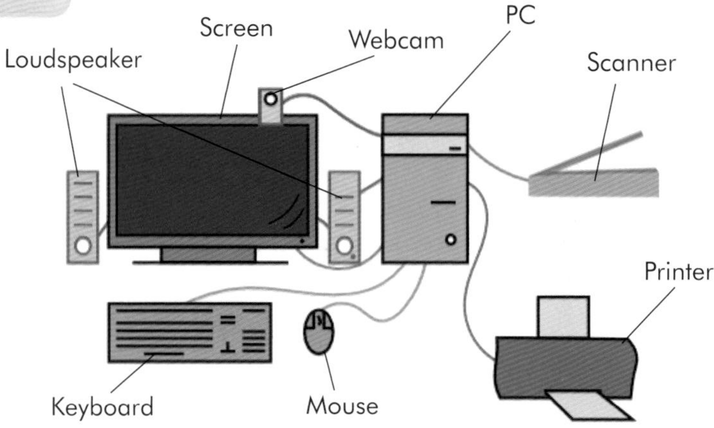

Peripheral devices are devices that can be connected to a computer via its ports. They are not part of the computer's processing unit.

Peripheral devices are elements external to a computer and are usually connected to the computer with a cable. The devices can also be connected using a Bluetooth connection (a kind of radio signal connection that works over short distances). Several kinds of input and output device exist. External hard disks, USB sticks, external drives, card readers or telephone headsets are all examples of peripheral devices.

Keyboards and computer mice (including joysticks) are input devices. They are used to send data to the central processor. A keyboard can have keys with letters, numbers and punctuation marks as well as an additional numeric keyboard. It also includes function keys and fields for controlling the cursor. A computer mouse relays the user's hand movements onto the screen. It enables the selection of commands and the movement of the symbols appearing on the screen. A synthetic mouse pad makes it easier to move the controlling ball on the base of a mouse. A joystick extends mouse function and makes it possible to manipulate several pictures at different speeds on the screen. They are mainly used in computer gaming.

Computer screens and printers are output devices.

The screen is a basic part of any computer. It displays texts, graphics, numbers etc. The printer transfers the data we see on screen onto paper or film. A printer driver converts the coded data in a computer into readable data. Different printer types include laser and inkjet printers. A scanner reads images and texts from books and transfers them to a computer where they can be viewed or

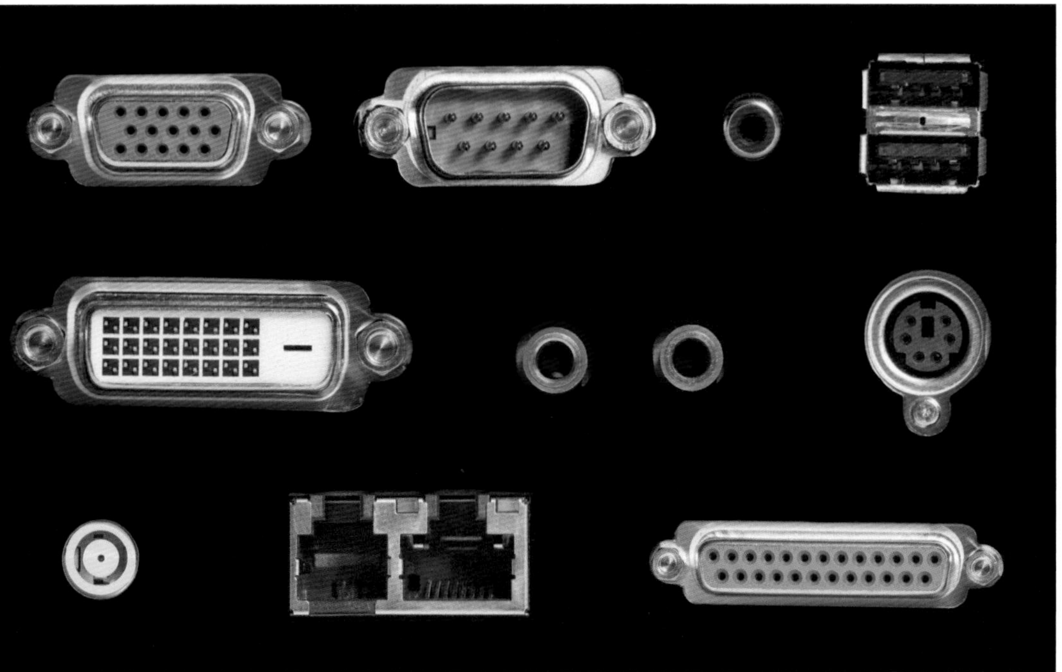

External devices are connected to computers via ports or interfaces. There are usually two USB ports, as on the top right. On the bottom right, in pink, is a parallel port, which used to be used mainly to connect a printer. In this context, 'parallel' refers to the fact that the data bits are transmitted in parallel via this connection, as opposed to a 'serial' port where the data bits are transmitted one after the other. In green you can see an old serial port with 9 poles. Modern USB ports are actually also serial interfaces because they transfer data in series. The name makes this clear: USB stands for Universal Serial Bus.
The blue port is the VGA or video graphics array port, via which a monitor or television can be connected; at the bottom, in the middle, are network/ethernet ports; the round black port with holes is an S-Video port (for 'separate' or 'super' video) through with information about brightness and colour is sent separately in order to improve picture quality.

If a computer doesn't have enough USB ports for all the external devices needed, a USB hub can solve the problem by providing extra ports.

worked on. When an object is scanned, a light beam scans every part of it before digitising it and sending it to a computer.

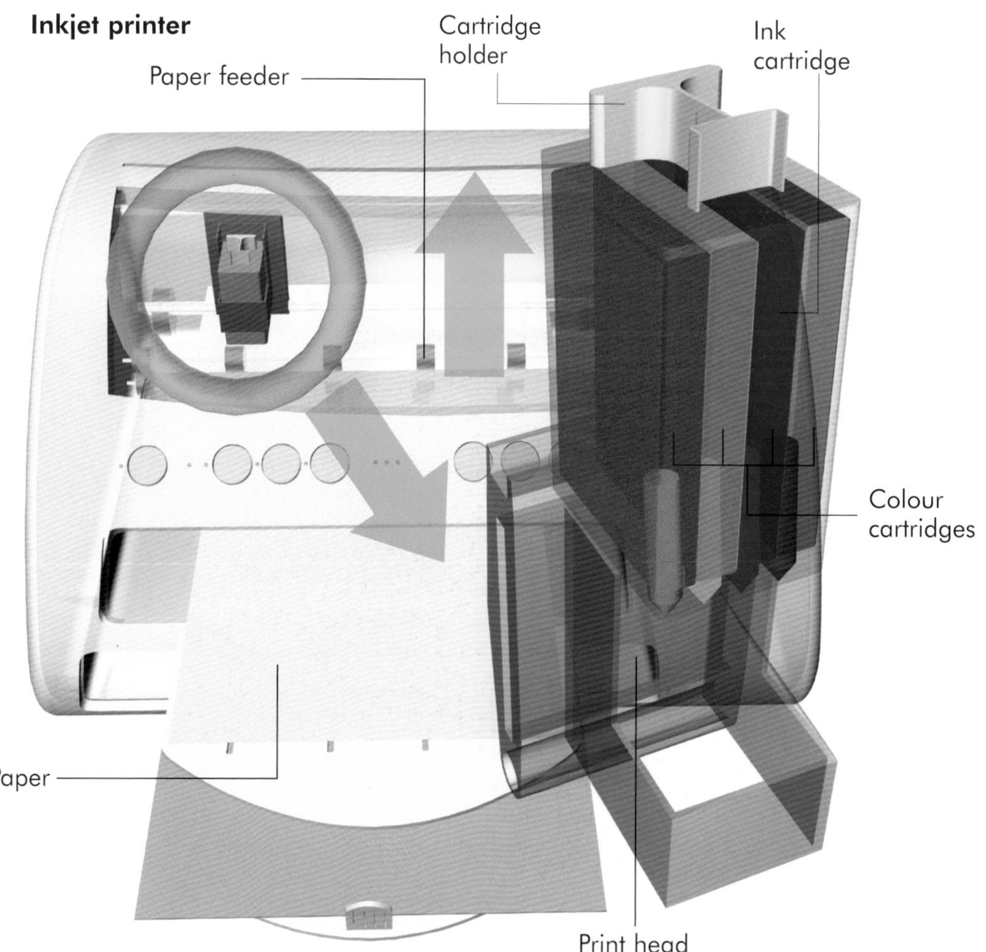

Inkjet printers *print with near photographic quality. Colour printing involves the use of a combination of several colour cartridges with the basic primary colours and black.*

The Internet

The Internet is available in even the most remote areas of the world, even without a personal computer.

The Internet is the biggest worldwide computer network. It connects millions of people to each other and is used to exchange information.

The origins of the Internet go back to 1969, to a computer network of the American defence ministry known as ARPANET. The main network of the Internet today developed out of ARPANET as the network expanded into private and public domains. The Internet can be accessed by several different

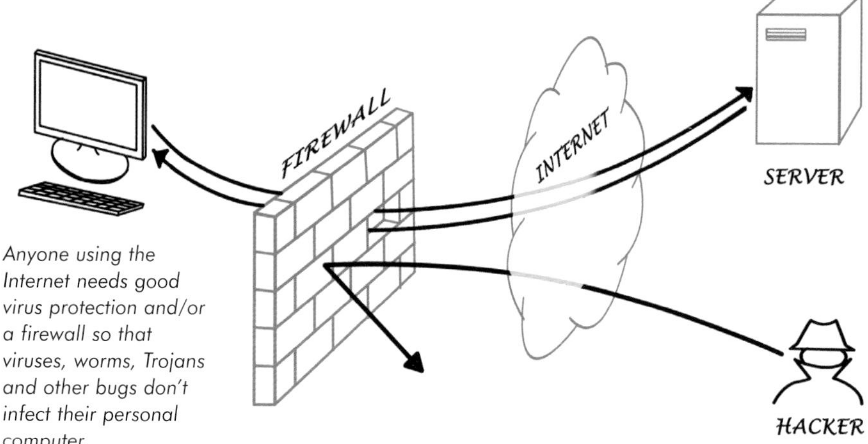

Anyone using the Internet needs good virus protection and/or a firewall so that viruses, worms, Trojans and other bugs don't infect their personal computer.

There has been an ever-increasing number of websites in the 'Net' since the mid-1990s. It is a mass of information that is difficult to structure or control. Search engines help us find the information we are looking for.

computers and through media such as telephone lines, satellites and fibre optic cables, all using a common transmission standard.

The Internet is made up of several decentralised networks but is the biggest single network in existence. There is no one single 'central control' that organises everything, instead a few big Internet providers manage the data traffic from their clients' computers, which are connected to large central servers. The data 'motorways' with huge capacity are usually powerful fibre optic cables known as 'backbones'. Whenever data is sent through these cables, whether that is e-mails or simply information relating to someone browsing an Internet page, data has to reach the user. The data is divided up into individual data packets and then sent to the destination via different routes. This ensures that the data arriving is always usable. Every packet knows the IP address of the destination computer where the packets will be reassembled.

The Internet's global breakthrough was only possible with the emergence of the World Wide Web in 1989, along with the invention of the programming language known as HTML (Hypertext Markup Language) and the spread of Web browsers – programs capable of representing HTML as Internet pages.

In HTML, 'normal' text is embedded with 'mark-up' or labels that instruct the text on how it should appear. For example, a line might tell the words 'tickets here' that the words should link directly to the page with tickets when clicked. Internet surfing is only possible with such hyperlink functions.

In the form of social media, the Internet has offered an abundance of opportunities for social intereaction since the beginning of this millennium. We can all join social networks, write blogs and contribute to online dictionaries as well as forums, exchange videos and photos, and listen to podcasts.

CHAPTER 9

Everyday life

The story of humankind is also the story of an unending stream of inventions. With our ability to think, we humans have the ability to develop things to help make life easier. Modern life is characterised by machines, homes with the comforts of electricity and heating, leisure and entertainment using telephones and other means of communication, and travel in all sorts of ways.

We use so many things on a daily basis without considering what went into their making. We write letters, use the telephone, heat our homes, use numerous kitchen gadgets and drive cars. We only think about how something works when something goes wrong with it. Only then do we see the complexities involved.

When we try to understand these complexities we can discover the interesting and varied nature of the world of optics, acoustics, mechanics or electricity. It becomes clear that many machines and gadgets work along similar principles or include a combination of different technologies.

Ballpoint and fountain pens

Ballpoint and fountain pens made it much easier to write and draw.

Important events and stories were recorded using pictures as long ago as ancient Egypt. A very fine papyrus stem or reed was used for writing. The Romans used metal styli. In the Middle Ages goose quills were used to write on papyrus or parchment. Special metal styli, usually made from steel that could be moistened with ink for writing, were only developed at the beginning of the 19th century. Ink pens used today are similar: the ink supply is kept in a refillable tube or replaceable cartridge inside the pen's holder.

Pressure is applied to the tip of the pen during writing to make the ink flow via a fine channel or capillaries below the nib. If pressure applied is increased the elastic slit in the pen's nib widens and more ink flows out and the writing strokes become broader.

The ballpoint pen is a different kind of writing implement. These robust pens have mini rolling balls at the tip. Their ink holders are usually filled with a kind of colour paste that flows out onto paper when the balls on the tip roll about. If the pens aren't held upright the ink supply is shut off and the pen is protected from drying out. The pens' tips are often retractable when the pens are not in use. Depending on the model, a spring in the pen's casing makes it possible to retract or release the pen tip by either clicking or twisting the top or end of the pen. Inkball pens work in a similar way to ballpoint pens, but they are filled with ink rather than paste.

How a piston fountain pen works

The ink supply is kept in a cylindrical barrel in the pen's handle. A piston in the barrel moves up and down when operated by a spindle. When the pen is dipped into the inkpot the piston is pulled up and draws ink into the barrel. The pen can then be used by applying variable pressure to the nib to make thick and thin lines.

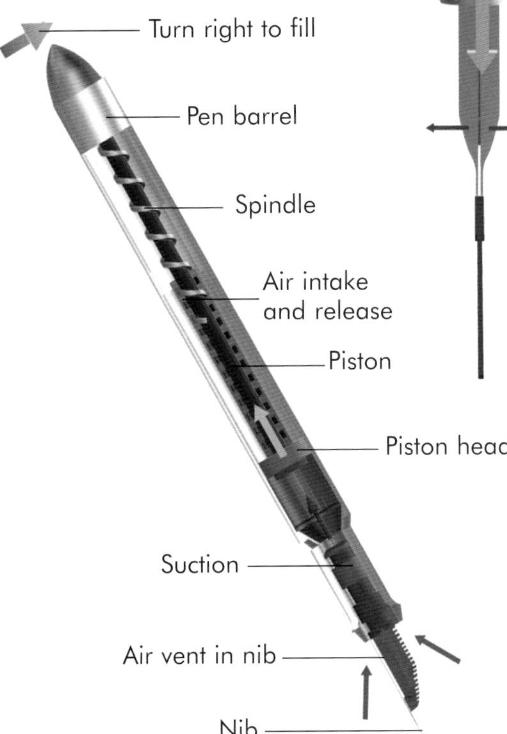

In early times goose quills were dipped in ink to write on paper.

Pocket watch

Fountain pens have long since dispensed with inkpots and springs, but they continue to be used in calligraphy.

Clocks and watches

A clock is a wheel-driven mechanism used to keep time. Clocks let us know the time of day but, depending on the model, they can also tells us the date, indicating year, day or month. One of the oldest ways of keeping time is the sundial. About 5,000 years old, its earliest form consisted of a staff or rod stuck in the earth to cast a shadow. Water clocks with a small hole from or into which water flowed were used from about 1400 BC. These were still being used in households until the 15th century. Candle clocks with markings to indicate hours were used from about AD 875. As the candle burned you could read the time on the markings. Wheel clocks came into use at end of the 13th century. Some cogwheels were about a metre in diameter and were placed in towers in front of castles and churches.

Modern clocks make use of a variety of mechanisms. Mechanical clocks derive their energy from a weight or a spring. To run steadily, the weight, usually a pendulum, has to be raised and the spring has to be wound tight. Interlocking gears drive the movement of a mechanical clock, while a pendulum or a 'balance wheel' mark time. Electrical clocks run on small battery- or solar-powered motors that deliver an alternating current at precise intervals. Quartz clocks have a tiny ring of quartz connected to a small electrical circuit that creates electronic oscillations at a precise frequency. A good quartz clock will keep time to within a second over a period of ten years. Atomic clocks use the oscillating frequencies of atoms to keep time and are used in physics research. The time it takes a particular atom, usually caesium-133, to swing between two energetic objects is used to mark time. An atomic clock loses time by as little as one second in three million years.

Gear movement

Mainspring (wound up as energy input)

Gears regulate the energy released

Potential energy in the spring is converted into movement of the clock hands

Mechanical clocks
The clock hands are driven by a mechanism that moves at a steady speed. The minute hand is regulated directly by a driving wheel. Two additional gear wheels drive the hour hand but slow down its rotation by a twelfth. The rotational speed of the driving wheel is regulated by an escape wheel connected to an anchor wheel. An anchor that moves in time with the balance wheel drives the anchor wheel. The balance wheel is driven in turn by the balance spring that has to be wound at regular intervals.

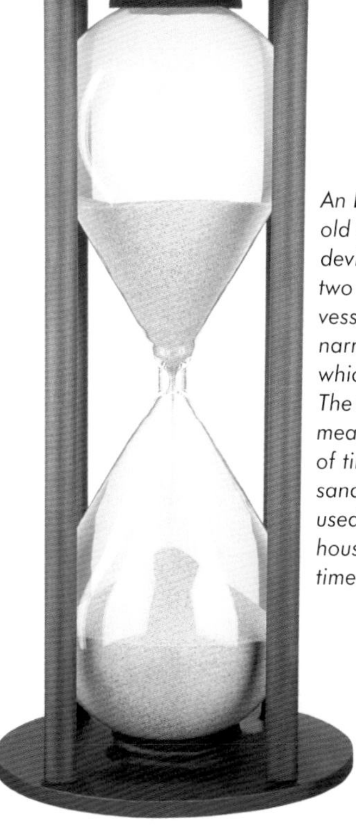

An ***hourglass*** *is a very old time-keeping device. It consists of two bulbous glass vessels connected by a narrow opening through which sand can trickle. The trickling sand measures the passage of time. Hour- or sandglasses are still used in saunas or households (as egg timers, for example).*

Washing machines

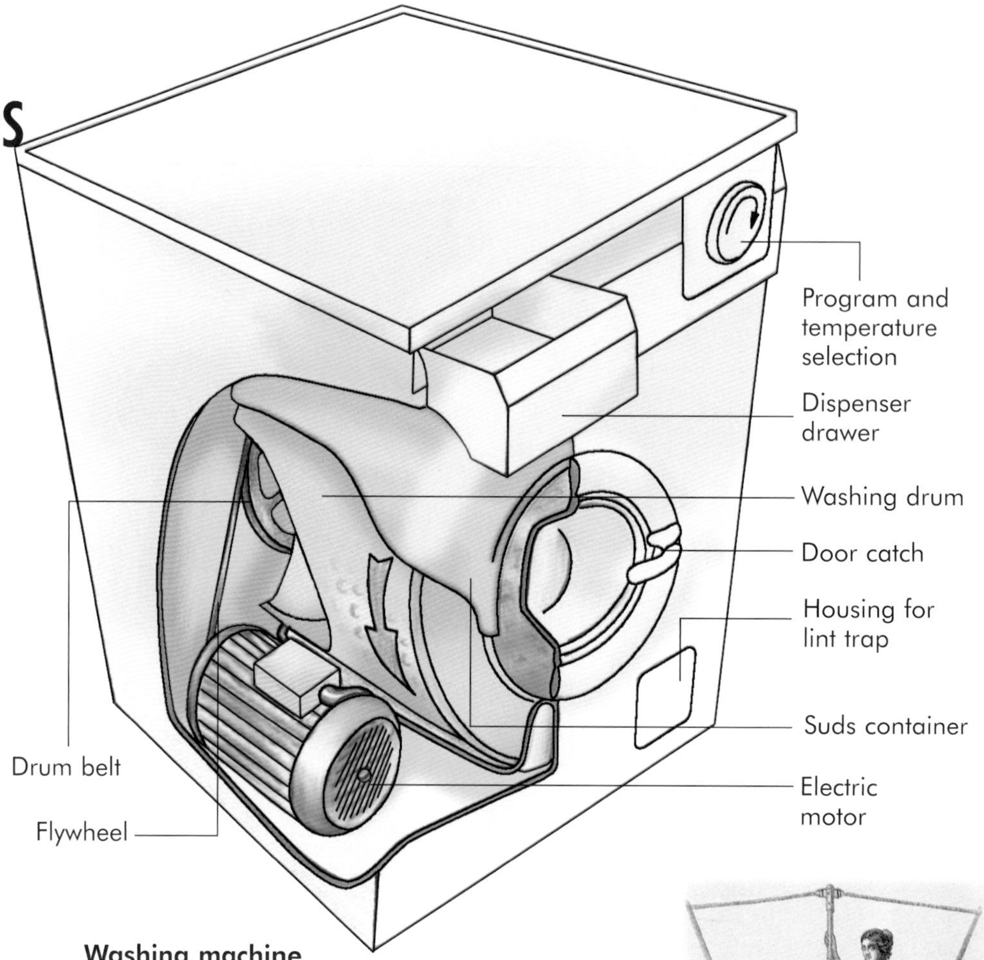

Washing machines are used to launder soiled textiles with heated water and detergent.

Fully automatic washing machines have taken away the arduous business of washing clothes by hand or by using a washboard. Most washing machines have ribbed and perforated stainless steel drums that hold the washing. The drum revolves alternately to the left and right within a soapy suds container that surrounds it.

The wash programme is operated by an electronic control that selects a programme depending on the size of the load, the nature of the textiles and how soiled the wash is, thereby saving energy, water and detergent. The loaded washing is cleaned by the drum's rolling movements and by being rubbed against the ribs of the drum. The program selected determines the amount of water and detergent released into the suds container. A magnetic valve controls the inflow of fresh water and detergent. A pipe connected to the suds container regulates the amounts. Once the flow of water is shut off, the heating element below the suds container switches on. A temperature gauge measures the temperature and switches the heating element off depending on the program selected.

The drum is driven by an electric motor. In a delicate cycle, the number of revolutions is much lower than during a spin cycle. The lint trap catches tiny bits of material that come off during a washing cycle.

Washing machine components

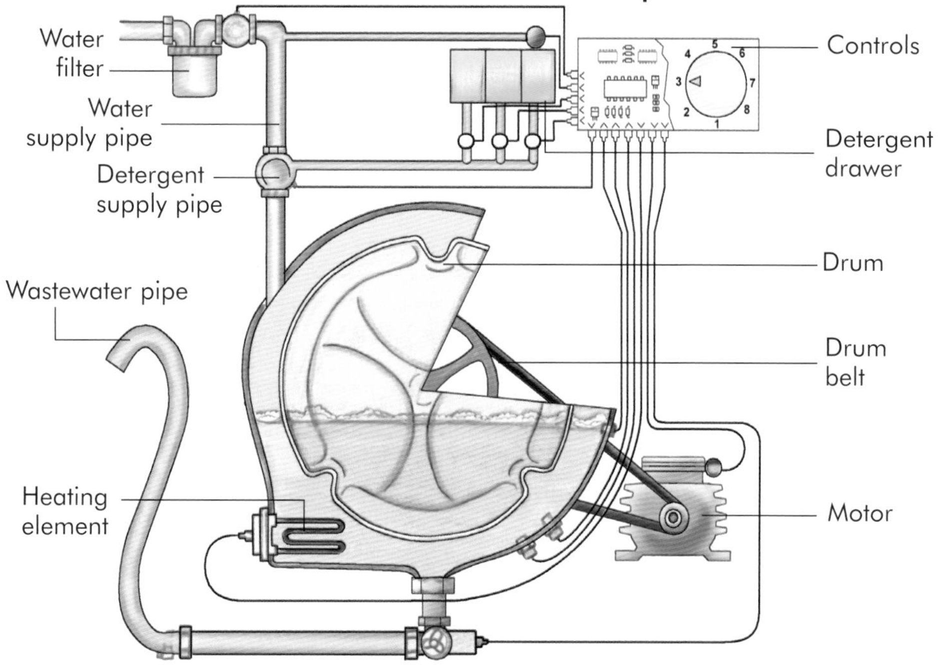

American washing machine, around 1850

Refrigerators

Refrigerators or 'fridges' are used to store food and keep it cool. Evaporating coolants known as refrigerants create the cool temperature that is needed.

People have always been conserving food by cooking, fermenting, drying or cooling. In earlier times, blocks of ice had to be used to cool food that might spoil easily.

Modern refrigerators create cold conditions by using electricity and a special coolant. Specific laws of physics govern the cooling process: during the process of evaporation every liquid absorbs heat and then releases it when it turns back into liquid from vapour.

In a refrigerator heat is moved from one place to another. A coolant with a low boiling point is circulated by means of a compressor. The coolant circulates in a piping system that runs from top to bottom at the back of the refrigerator. Previously used CFC coolants have now been replaced with more environmentally friendly versions.

The coolant circulating in the pipes gets hot as it absorbs heat from inside the refrigerator. The vapour created by this process is compressed by a compressor, and turns into highly compressed gas. A condenser then releases the heat absorbed from inside the refrigerator into the air outside. The piping system at the back of the refrigerator is the condenser. The back of the refrigerator should be well ventilated to avoid a build-up of heat.

As the gas cools it liquefies. The coolant then flows through a capillary tube – an expansion valve – that prevents a pressure balance occurring between the condenser and evaporator. The coolant goes back into the evaporator or compressor and the cycle begins again.

Air currents created by differences in temperature distribute the cool temperatures inside the refrigerator. Thermostats and pumps circulate the coolant at different rates to regulate the temperature inside the refrigerator.

Refrigerator casing is usually made from highly insulating polyurethane foam, which is also able to withstand high pressure.

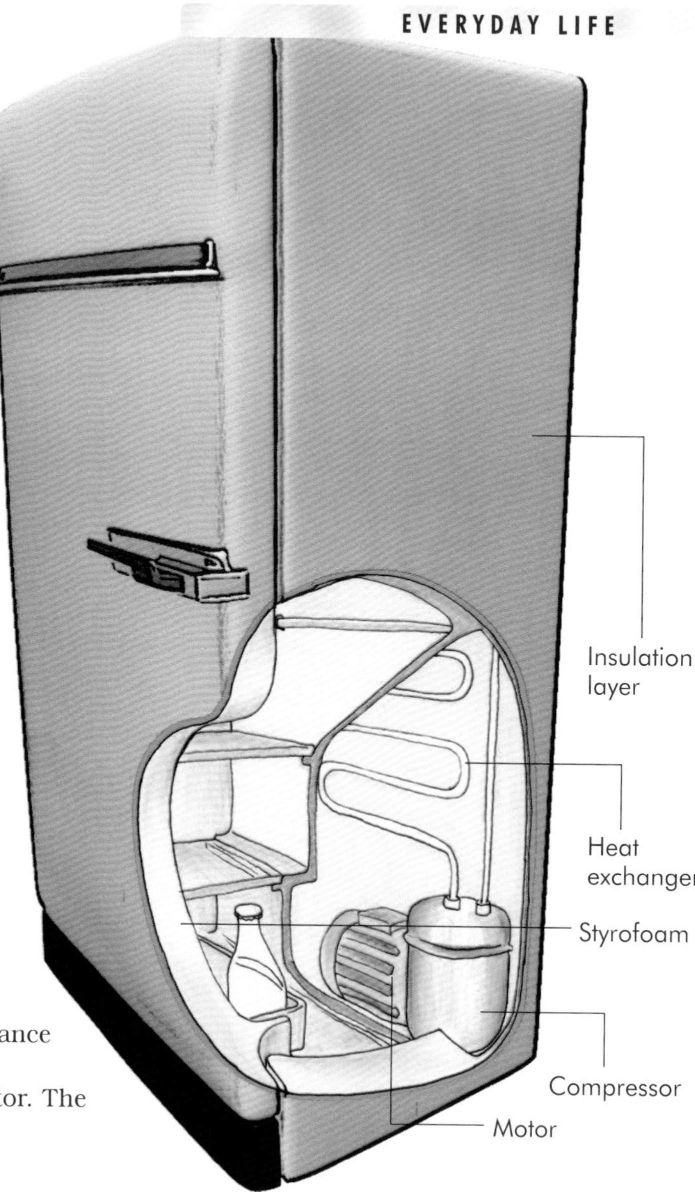

***Refrigerators** have an insulating outer casing that stops air getting inside. The inside of a refrigerator is made of a synthetic material, the outer casing is metal with a thick insulating layer in between usually made of Styrofoam.*

Diagram illustrating the cooling cycle

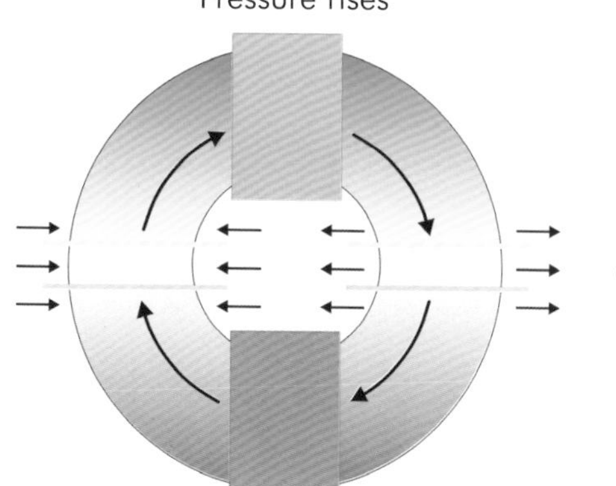

Vacuum cleaners

A vacuum cleaner is an electrical device used to remove dust and other dirt particles from carpets, floors and furniture in domestic and commercial buildings.

The main part of a vacuum cleaner is made up of a cylinder with a fan and a motor. The electric motor drives the fan and a vacuum is created. Air outside the cylinder is sucked in, taking in dust and dirt along with it. The dirt particles are caught in a paper bag inside the cylinder. The dirt stays here as if caught in a filter, while the air which has been cleansed of the dust and dirt leaves the cylinder through an exhaust. When the paper bag is full it can easily be removed and replaced.

Small upright vacuum cleaners are moved directly over dirty surfaces to clean floors, while cylinder vacuum cleaners have long tubes with a nozzle at the end. The tube is flexible and makes it possible to clean places that are hard to reach.

Upright vacuum cleaners often have special heads, such as brushes, designed to clean particular surfaces (carpets, hard floors, furniture). Specific shampooing devices are used to spread detergents on badly soiled areas that can then be vacuum cleaned. Special wet–dry vacuum cleaners can even vacuum liquids.

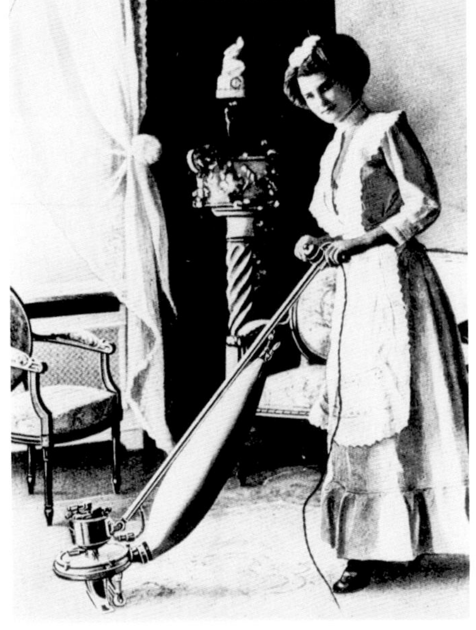

Vacuum cleaner model from 1911
The first carpet cleaners didn't suck in the dust but blew it off instead. Actual suction vacuum cleaners first appeared around 1900.

Controls on the cleaner regulate the suction power needed to vacuum depending on the area that needs cleaning.

Modern vacuum cleaners using cyclone technology no longer use bags. Instead they catch the dust, which has already been separated from the air, in a container, while the clean air is blown out again. The cleaner maintains its suction power regardless of how full or empty the container is.

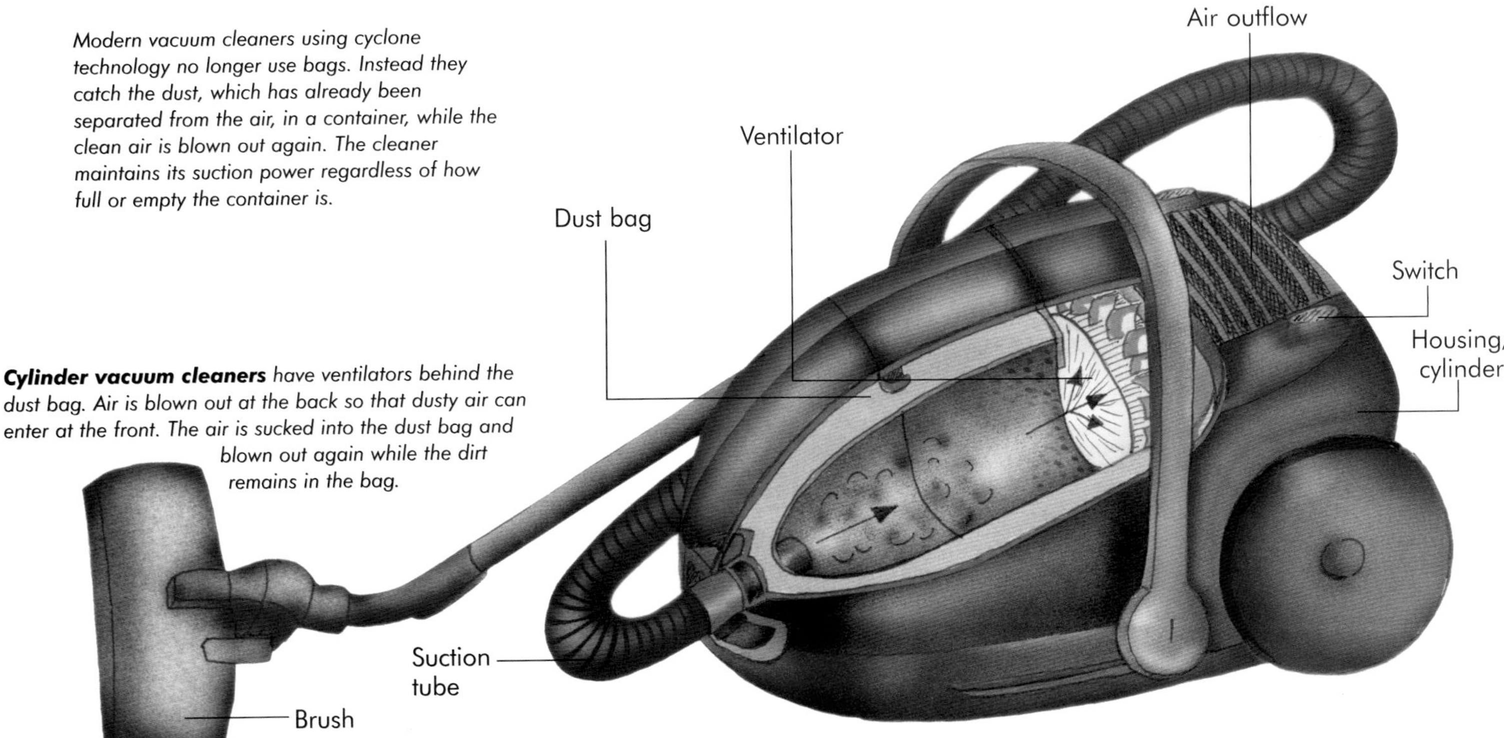

Cylinder vacuum cleaners *have ventilators behind the dust bag. Air is blown out at the back so that dusty air can enter at the front. The air is sucked into the dust bag and blown out again while the dirt remains in the bag.*

Telephones

Telephones enable communication over long distances by converting speech vibrations into electrical signals and back into speech.

Alexander Graham Bell (1847–1922) is credited with inventing the telephone in 1876. A German teacher called Philipp Reis was, however, the first to demonstrate that sound could be converted into electrical oscillations. Bell made use of this principle to develop an early telephone. In 1880 the German company Siemens made further improvements to the technology. The development of automatic telephonic transmission and amplifier tubes made communication over long distances possible and in 1928 the first long distance call between Germany and America took place.

Mobiles

For a telephone to work you need mechanisms that will convert signals, transmit an electrical signal to both speakers, and then convert the electrical signals back into speech vibrations. For your voice to be carried you have to speak into the mouthpiece of a phone which holds a small carbon microphone. The tiny carbon granules in the microphone are pressed together at different rates by a metallic membrane activated by the speech/sound vibrations. This induces changes in the electrical current in the phone line. The resulting current fluctuations are amplified and transmitted through cables. The electrical impulses are then converted back as they arrive at the receiver's end. The incoming impulses make an electromagnet vibrate in synch with another magnet. The electrical signals are then converted into audible sound signals through a membrane in the receiver.

Several years ago carbon microphones began to be replaced by piezoelectric microphones using crystals instead of carbon granules.

Parts of a telephone receiver

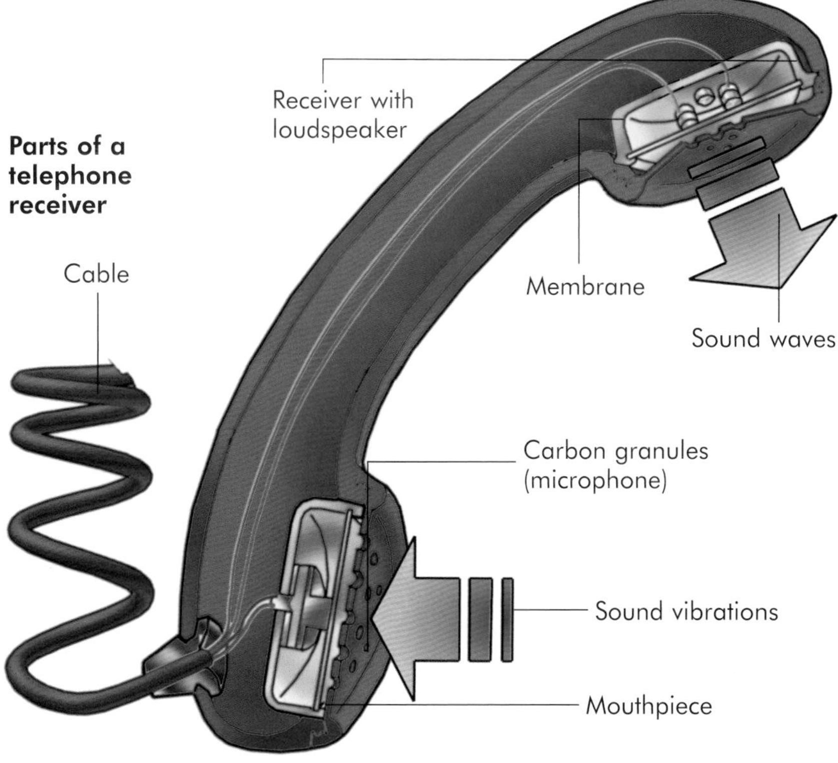

*The first **telephone with a rotary dial** was used in 1896 in the town hall in Milwaukee. The dial was turned using 'lugs' on the fingerplate. Holes in the dial came later.*

Cordless telephones are the norm today and they make it much easier to have conversations within a specific distance from a base station without having to use cables. Most people also use a mobile telephone that can be used anywhere at any time as a phone, and to surf the Internet, take photos and much more. Using the Internet to make calls is another good option, and if the person you are speaking to has a webcam you can even see each other.

Practical and widespread since the arrival of the smartphone: using the Internet on a mobile phone is a good way of finding the restaurant you are looking for while on holiday.

GLOSSARY

Acid rain
Rain with high levels of acid arising from the formation of sulphuric acid from incineration plants, but also from nitrogen oxides from exhaust fumes.

Aerodynamics
The study of how gases move.

Ampere
A, the unit of measurement for electrical currents.

Analog–digital converter
An analog-to-digital converter turns and transmits the voltage of information (e.g. input signals in an electrical current) from analog form into digital form.

ARPANET
'Advanced Research Projects Agency Network': an experimental network from the early 1970s created by the US Department of Defense. The software and basic concepts of today's Internet originated here. ARPANET no longer exists.

ASCII
'American Standard Code for Information Interchange': a standardised code used in computers to represent specific information.

@ (at)
A symbol or sign that separates the name of the sender from the name of the provider in an e-mail address.

Atom
'Indivisible primary matter': in chemical terms, the smallest particle that cannot be split by a chemical process with the particle retaining the characteristics of its element. In physical terms, the smallest particle of an element with a nucleus and shell.

Axle
A spindle around which the wheels of a vehicle turn.

Betamax
A video recording format developed by Sony in 1976 and since replaced by the VHS format.

Bilge pump
A pump used to pump out seawater from the widest part of a ship above the keel.

Boltrope
The rope that is stitched to the edge of every sail using flat stiches. The different sides and edges of the sail are known as the luff, leech, foot and head.

Bow
The forward part of a ship or boat.

Buffer
An intermediate storage area for data to balance out the reduced speed of peripheral devices.

Bulkheads
Horizontal or vertical steel partitions used in ships, mainly to organise space but also to stabilise and safeguard a ship in case of leaks or fire.

Cache
In computing, an intermediate storage area where frequently used data is stored so it can be retrieved quickly.

Cam
A mechanical part consisting of a shaft connected to an off-centre disc, and used to convert rotary (turning) movement into reciprocating (back and forth) movement.

Camshaft
An essential component of engine control in a cylinder head; in particular, it controls the valves.

CCD
'Charge-coupled device': a semi-conductor device that converts incoming light into an equivalent number of free electrons that are then turned into digital signals.

Celluloid
Elastic, transparent, easily combustible synthetic material that was once used to make films.

CFC
Chlorofluorocarbon: gases or liquids used as coolants in air conditioners and refrigerators as well as a propellant in aerosols. The use of CFCs is now being limited because they are very damaging to the atmosphere's ozone layer.

Cleats
Sail supports on ships and boats.

Coil
A wound, conductive wire, with at least one winding. Current running through a coil will create an electromagnetic field.

Connecting rod
A connecting rod flexibly connects a piston and crankshaft in such a way that the force from the piston's reciprocating movement can be converted into the crankshaft's rotary motion.

Crankshaft
A shaft attached to connecting rods with crank pins. A crankshaft converts the reciprocating motion of pistons and relays it as rotary motion.

Cubic capacity (engine displacement)
Cubic capacity is the volume

displaced by all the pistons of an engine between their turning points. The size of cylinders is usually expressed as their cubic capacity.

Cursor
An indicator: the blinking point on a computer screen that highlights where the next input into the computer will take place.

Differential
The part of a gear that ensures that the inner wheels of a car will turn more slowly than the outer wheels when the car makes a turn.

Dioptric
Dioptric means 'refracting' or 'transparent'. A diopter telescope has refracting elements such as lenses or prisms and beam limiting apertures.

D2-MAC System
'Duo binary coded Multiplex Analog Components' system was a transmission format proposed as the new unified norm for television in Europe intended to optimise transmission.

DVD-ROM
A readable but not rewritable storage disc with 4.7 to 17 GB capacity.

Four-wheel drive
In a four-wheel drive all four wheels are driven by engine power to create better traction between the wheels and the ground (for example in icy conditions).

Flatbed
Loading surface in a lorry.

Floating point unit (FPU)
An FPU is a coprocessor that makes calculations with floating point numbers to increase the speed of mathematical and graphic operations.

Foresail
A small, triangular sail that is not the mainsail.

Fuselage
The outside body of an aeroplane

Galley
A kitchen on an aeroplane or ship.

Generator
The generator of a car driven by the engine that creates electricity from mechanical energy.

Halogens
Compounds of fluorine, chlorine, bromine, iodine and astatine.

Hominids
Members of an order of living beings including human beings today and their ancestors, as well as great apes. Hominids are characterised by their ability to use tools and to walk erect.

Hub
The central part of a wheel running through the axle.

Hull
The outside body of a ship.

Keel
Stabilising structure along the bottom of a ship.

Log in
When you 'log in' you apply for and receive access to a network or mailbox by entering a username and password.

Modem
A signal converter that relays data between computer systems along a telephone line at an appropriate speed.

Mono
Recorded or replayed on a single channel.

Motherboard
The motherboard is a computer's largest circuit board, coated with a thin copper or silver plate with additional sockets.

NASA
'National Aeronautics and Space Administration': the American space agency founded by President Eisenhower in 1958.

O-ring chain
A drive chain used for transmission and consisting of two internal links with cylinders interlocking with two external links with pins.

Pixel
Short for 'picture element': the tiny points that make up an image on a screen. Pixels are the smallest elements in a raster display. The smaller the pixel, the higher and deeper the resolution of the image.

Plutonium
A radioactive chemical element used in nuclear bombs and power plants.

Port or interface
The point at which two devices are connected in order to exchange data, for example a computer and peripheral device.

Radar
'Radio detecting and ranging': a device used to send out focused electromagnetic rays whose reflections are then 'recaptured' in order to locate or measure something.

Radioactivity
Radiation released by the decay of atoms.

Read/write head
An electromagnet that can read, write and erase any part of a disc or hard drive.

Relay
An electronic component that works like a switch. It is switched on and off by a control circuit.

Reservoir
An artificial lake created to store water behind a dam.

Rim
The outer part of a wheel, usually made of metal, on which the tyre sits.

Satellite
Manmade object with no integral source of power, launched into outer space to orbit another natural body in space, usually the Earth. Examples include weather, communications and news and research satellites.

Server
The computer in a computer network that has specific functions such as the administration of data banks or hard drives, the running of the network itself or communication between other networks such as telephone lines.

Shadow mask
A plate with small holes through which electron beams can travel so as to create a pixel on a screen or monitor.

Shellac
A natural, yellowy resin, which was used to manufacture records. It is secreted by the female lac insect and is used today in sealants or furniture varnish.

Shock absorber
A hydraulic spring component used in cars to absorb strong movements and vibrations.

Space probe
An unmanned plane or spaceship used for the scientific exploration of the atmosphere and outer space.

Stator pack
A group of magnets that keep a Maglev train suspended.

Stereo
A system used to create more spacious sound – sounds are either recorded or replayed from two channels.

Stereoscopic
Giving the impression of spatial depth in a three-dimensional representation.

Stern
The back of a ship or vehicle

Stern propeller
A ship's propeller positioned at the stern that helps steer the ship.

Swash plate
A round disc mounted at an angle to its rotational axis. It is used in helicopters. When used in conjunction with a gear rod it can alter the position of the rotor blades.

Thermal
A rising mass of warm wind; updraught.

Torque (turning force or moment of force)
Torque is the amount of force that can be exerted on a rigid object. The force makes the object turn on its axis. In a car, the torque from the engine is transmitted to the wheels via the clutch and axle.

Track
Data track on an external storage device (hard disk, floppy disk) or CDs.

Tube
Mounting for the optical components in an optical device.

Turbine
A machine set in rotary motion by another source of energy (e.g. water, hot air, steam) to create mechanical energy.

Ultrasound
Sounds with a frequency higher than 20,000 Hz, not audible to the human ear.

VHS
'Video Home System': a video recording system dating from 1975 made by the Victor Company of Japan (JVC).

Volt
V, a unit of electric current. Voltage is the difference between the electric charges of two charge carriers (e.g. the poles of a battery). Depending on its nature, a current can be direct or alternating, of low or high voltage.

VR glasses
'Virtual reality' glasses: a device worn like conventional spectacles with a screen appearing in front of each eye showing computer-generated images.

Watt
W, a physical unit denoting work or energy undertaken or stopped in a given time frame.

INDEX

PHOTO AND ARTWORK CREDITS

Abbreviations used:
(a.) = above; (b.) = below; (c.) = centre; (r.) = right; (l.) = left

Lignite power station Neurath: p. 22 b.l.
Flickr: p. 59 a. (JVC America), 80 a. (Dnikolos), 82 a.l. (JonDissed)
Fotolia.com: p. 5 b. (© lexaarts), 17 l. (© typomaniac), 55 a. (© Maruba), 55 b. (© Spectral-Design), 59 b.l. (© RLG), 59 b.r. (© lionel VALENTI), 68 b. (© Peter Kirillov), 69 c. (© Roman Sigaev), 69 b. (© seen), 74 c. (© Eva Kahlmann), 74 b (© Beata Wojciechowska), 75 a.l. (© Nikolai Sorokin), 75 a.r. (© Claudio Bravo), 76 a. (© blende40), 77 a.l. (© Abel Tumik), 77 a.r. (© cspcreative), 77 c.l. (© Birgit Reitz-Hofmann), 77 c.r. (© seen), 77 b.l. (© Zauberhut), 77 b.r. (© krischam), 78 a (© Vtls), 79 a.l. (© Peter Atkins), 79 a.r. (© Mihai Simoni), 79 c. (© m.schuckart), 80 b. (© Stephen Coburn), 81 a. (© Anna Chelnokova), 82 a.r. (© HaywireMedia), 82 b.l. (© Dmitry), 82 b.r. (© Victoria), 83 b.r. (© vladgrin), 90 c. (© MP2), 91 a.l. (© lexaarts), 91 b.r. (© Ingo Bartussek)
Hendrik Kranenberg, Drolshagen: p. 78 b.
NASA: p. 42 b.l.
Wikimedia: p. 79 b. (Medvedev)
All other images:
Contramedia Ltd archive